. . .AND T
PRO
A New Prophe
Churc
by
Clifford and Monica Hill

Collins
MARSHALL PICKERING

William Collins Sons & Co. Ltd
London · Glasgow · Sydney · Auckland
Toronto · Johannesburg

First published in Great Britain in 1990 by Marshall Pickering

Marshall Pickering is an imprint of
Collins Religious Division,
part of the HarperCollins Publishing Group
8 Grafton Street, London W1X 3LA

Printed and bound in Great Britain by William Collins
Sons & Co. Ltd, Glasgow

CONTENTS

. . . AND THEY SHALL PROPHESY!

Dr Clifford Hill is founder and director of
Prophetic Word Ministries and a recognised authority
on prophecy. He is editor-in-chief of the magazine
Prophecy Today. His many books include the recently
published *Prophecy- Past and Present*.
Mrs Monica Hill is Executive Officer of the British
Church Growth Association. She is editor of *The Church
Growth Digest* which examines trends in the Church
today, and is author of *Rich Christians,
Poor Christians*.

The royalties from this book are being donated to the
establishment of a School of Ministry with an emphasis
on the biblical basis of prophecy.
Further information can be obtained by writing to: PWM
Trust, Nasmith House, 175 Tower Bridge Road, London
SE1 2AB.

Authors' Preface

Throughout our marriage, while raising our three children, we have found opportunities for working together in developing a partnership ministry using the different gifts God has given us. We had a long and fruitful ministry in the East End of London working among the poor and the immigrants, developing new concepts of urban mission and renewal in an inner city context during which Monica was responsible for reopening three redundant churches and Clifford developed an increasingly prophetic edge to his ministry. Although today we each have our particular responsibilities in church growth and prophecy we find many opportunities of ministering together both in Britain and in other parts of the world.

Our first reaction when we were asked to write this book was to reject it as not being right for us, but as we prayed about it we realised that we have been seeing the evidence of a new prophetic movement as we have travelled worldwide ministering in different nations. We felt that God was urging us to share the vision of what we ourselves have experienced. We have brought together the different insights of both the prophetic/evangelistic ministry and church growth.

Although we have each been responsible for a number of books and we each edit Christian magazines, this is our first joint book and we have enjoyed the experience of writing it together. We trust this will be an encouragement to other married couples who have similarly been led into a partnership of ministry. Personal experiences of prophetic ministry throughout the book are Clifford's and are written in the first person singular. These have been indented to show that they are his, rather than our joint, writing.

It is our hope that this book, with its many first-hand accounts of the wonderful things that God is doing among his people, will be an encouragement to all readers. Our prayer is that this will stimulate further searching of the scriptures which will lead to fresh experiences of the love and presence of the Lord Jesus who is pouring out his Spirit in great abundance today.

Clifford and Monica Hill
September 1990

Chapter One

The God Who Fulfils His Promises

These are exciting days in which to be a Christian! Everywhere you look there is evidence that God is at work.

Of course, that could be said of every generation. There never has been a time when God was not at work. He existed before the beginning of time. He created the universe. He formed the world out of the void and he sustains it by his power. He created men and women in his own image for fellowship with himself. From earliest times he began revealing his purposes, his nature and his ways to his people. He spoke to them directly through his servants the prophets and in every generation he has never left himself without a witness.

The Significance of this Present Age

So what is special about our generation? Is there some particular significance in the things that are happening in our own lifetime? Clearly we live in the most amazing times.

The speed of change is bewildering in every sphere of life. People who have lived through the Twentieth

Century have witnessed the greatest period of change in the entire history of the world. There have been amazing changes in technology. The everyday household gadgets we use today would have been considered science fiction at the beginning of the century. The economic changes have also been phenomenal. They have brought incredible wealth to some and grinding poverty to others. The social changes, especially in the western nations, have transformed society from the dominance of age and tradition to the dominance of youth and pop culture. The moral code that has held the family and society stable for centuries has been overturned in a single lifetime. Even in the world of nature there have been significant changes in the world's weather patterns, exacerbated by the environmental problems of pollution, global warming and destruction of natural resources, that have occupied the attention of scientists throughout the world.

Probably the most astounding changes, however, have been reserved for the end of the century. These are the political changes that are still occurring. The changes in Eastern Europe that took place in 1989 were seen to signal the break-up of the apparently impregnable Communist Empire led by the Soviet Union. Headline writers simply ran out of superlatives as one change followed another, including the fall of the Berlin Wall that heralded the end of the Cold War and the end of an era.

All these changes, together with the heightening tension in the Middle East since the establishment of the State of Israel in 1948 and the Six Day War that restored Jerusalem to the Jews in 1967, have caused those who are familiar with biblical prophecy to ask the question "Are we approaching the last days?" In order to answer this question we need to examine what the Bible actually says.

There is a prophecy in Haggai (2:6–7) that speaks

of God shaking the nations and the whole created order as a prelude to filling his house with glory. This same prophecy is repeated in Hebrews 12:26f where the interpretation is given that when God moves in power to shake the whole created order and to shake the nations, he will be preparing the way for the coming kingdom of Christ on earth. He will do this by shaking all the established social, political, economic and natural systems upon which men and women put their trust. We will refer to these prophecies in more detail in the next chapter. There are certainly many indications that an unprecedented shaking of the nations and the whole of nature is taking place today.

"In the Last Days"

The signs of the end of the age that Jesus gave his disciples, listed in Matthew 24 and Luke 21, can all be seen happening today. Probably the most important prophetic landmark is the restoration of the Jews to their ancient home land and the control of Jerusalem. Jesus' own reference to the letter was in an eschatological context as preceding his own Second Coming (Luke 21:24).

The rapid succession of events in the second half of the Twentieth Century, that bear remarkable resemblance to events described in biblical prophecy as pertaining to "the last days", have given rise to much speculation. Numerous books have been published forecasting the imminence of the Rapture of the church, the battle of Armageddon and even dating the end of the world.

These speculations have little value in terms of biblical scholarship and have done much to give prophecy a bad name. What is most needed today is a sober reflection on the evidence of what is now happening in the world in the light of the word of God in scripture and all that we know of the nature and purposes of God. We need to leave aside the world of fantasy and Hollywood-style science fiction views of eschatology and study carefully what the Bible actually says about the last days.

It needs to be noted that when Jesus spoke of "the last days" he was not referring to the end of the world but to a particular period in history associated with his own Messianic mission. The Messianic Age is spoken of throughout scripture as a time when God will establish his reign upon the earth. It will be inaugurated by Christ himself returning to this earth.

If we are, in fact, drawing near to that time, we need to be aware of it. Although Jesus warned us not to forecast dates and times, he did say that we should be alert and prepared. We are to be a watching, praying people. Being prepared is important, as Jesus made clear in several of his parables, for example, that of the wise and foolish virgins (Matthew 25:1–13). Jesus followed this with the parable of the talents (vv. 14–30), reminding us that we are here for a purpose and we will be accountable to him for how we have lived our lives. Jesus, himself, was able to say to his Father at the end of his life "I have brought you glory on earth by completing the work you gave me to do" (John 17:4).

Clearly, if we knew we were going to die tonight, we would spend the day rapidly completing unfinished tasks we believed to have been given to us by the Lord (or at least ensuring that they would be passed on to others for completion). We would also see that our personal affairs were in order, throwing out the junk, and probably setting right some relationships that had gone wrong. Alternatively, if we knew we were to receive a visit from an honoured guest, we would not only prepare ourselves, we would also clean the house, prepare a room, prepare food and we would also prepare other members of the family to ensure that they too were ready to receive him.

If we are indeed entering the "last days" of this present age, we need to understand what that means so that we can rightly be prepared to respond to the purposes of God for our lives.

It is not the purpose of this book to examine the wide variety of "signs of the times" that are occurring in the contemporary world. It is our purpose to examine just one of them – the rise of a prophetic movement – a new awareness that God is speaking to his people today, and that we are witnessing the emergence of a prophetic people. This was what was foreseen by the prophet Joel.

> "And afterwards, I will pour out my Spirit on all people. Your sons and daughters will prophesy, your old men will dream dreams, your young men will see visions. Even on my servants, both men and women, I will pour out my Spirit in those days" (Joel 2:28–29).

This was repeated by Peter on the day of Pentecost. John Stott says that Peter "deliberately changes Joel's 'afterwards' (as the time when the Spirit will be poured out) to 'in the last days' in order to emphasise that with the Spirit's coming the last days have come" (John Stott, *The Message of Acts*, IVP, 1990, p73) That overlooks the point that Joel was using a Hebrew idiom which had eschatological significance. Peter deliberately transferred this from its Hebrew code language into ordinary everyday terms that could be understood by a multi-cultural audience. But John Stott is perfectly right in saying that Peter was declaring that the age of fulfilment had begun on that very day. The day of Pentecost, the Jewish feast of the first fruits of the harvest, inaugurated the Messianic era. Stott is also right in warning that we must not misinterpret Peter's words to imply that he thought the great outpouring of the Spirit was going to be at some future point "for this is not how Peter understood and applied the text. The whole Messianic age, which stretches between the two comings of Christ, is the age of the Spirit in which his ministry is one of abundance" (ibid).

That is perfectly true but it would not be true to say that the abundance of the outpouring of the Holy Spirit has been seen equally in every generation. Church history, as Latourette has shown, reveals that the growth of the Church has not been one of uniform steady expansion. The growth pattern has been in waves, with ebb and flow, recession and advance. Each advance, however, has been larger than the previous one and each recession is smaller, so that with each fresh wave of the Spirit a new high-water mark is reached. The Church is currently experiencing a period of tremendous worldwide growth that looks set to continue into the Twenty-First Century bringing multitudes into the kingdom.

Joel's prophecy speaks of the Spirit of God being "poured out" which suggests a tremendous deluge, not just a gentle rain, and we believe that what we are seeing today is very much in keeping with Joel's vision.

That vision also foresaw the superabundance of the Spirit being poured out upon "all people" but this does not mean the whole population of the world irrespective of their spiritual condition – it means irrespective of worldly distinctions such as sex (your sons and daughters), age (your young men and your old men) and social rank (even on my servants). God's promise was to bestow his Spirit upon all those who were open to receive him and, as Peter made clear later in his first sermon in Jerusalem, it meant those who were in a right relationship with God through repentance and being baptised into Christ. "Repent and be baptised, every one of you, in the name of Jesus Christ, so that your sins may be forgiven. And you will receive the gift of the Holy Spirit" (Acts 2:38).

Peter added to the prophecy of Joel the words "And they will prophesy" in order to stress the significance of the inauguration of the Messianic era. The dawn of the age of the Spirit meant that every Spirit-filled believer would be able to prophesy. It was for this reason that Paul urged all the believers in Corinth to "eagerly desire spiritual gifts, especially the gift of prophecy" (1 Corinthians 14:1). This did not, of course, mean that either Peter or Paul expected every one to be called into the ministry of the prophet but they did realise that each one could and should exercise the *gift* of prophecy. Prophecy thus understood here is in its basic biblical context and simply means the discerning and declaring of the word of God in the contemporary situation.

It was Moses who first gave voice to the wish that all God's people should be prophets (Numbers 11:29) but he realised that for this to happen the Spirit of God would have to fall upon all of them. Clearly he was expressing the heart of God in this because centuries later Isaiah received a promise that this was precisely what God intended to do, "I will pour out my Spirit on your offspring and my blessing on your descendants" (Isaiah 44:3). Isaiah perceived God doing this in the same way as he poured out a deluge of water on the thirsty land and filled the streams across the parched ground. He foresaw the coming age of the Spirit transforming the world in the same way as a prolonged downpour of rain after a long drought changes the entire countryside. The brown dried-up valley of death becomes a green fertile place of new life.

Jeremiah foresaw this promise being fulfilled, when God would establish a "new covenant" with his people which would enable each one to know him personally and to enter into a right relationship with him. He heard God declare "they will all know me from the least of them to the greatest" (Jeremiah 31:34).

Joel had the same vision of all God's people, regardless of age, sex or status, coming to know him in a new way through the action of God himself pouring out his Spirit upon them. It was precisely this that Peter and the disciples of Jesus experienced at Pentecost. Peter tried to describe to the people of Jerusalem what had happened to them, assuring them that this could also be their own experience. He declared that God had promised that the power which he and the 120 believers had received was available to everyone who would repent and believe (Acts 2:38).

The Age of the Spirit

Peter must have been greatly encouraged when three thousand people responded to the first preaching of the Gospel message but there were many more who did not respond. Jerusalem was filled to capacity for the Festival with pilgrims from many different parts of the world. Luke records that many of these visitors heard the message in their own languages and it is reasonable to assume that some of them would be numbered among those baptised that day.

It seems clear that a Hellenist Messianic church was formed in Jerusalem from the earliest times as indicated by the dispute that arose over caring for the widows (Acts 6) and the Greek names of "the Seven" who were appointed by the apostles. The disciples openly witnessed to the resurrection of Jesus and preached the Gospel even in the precincts of the temple. The miraculous power God had bestowed upon them through the outpouring of the Holy Spirit was demonstrated for all to see in the healing of the lame man at "the temple gate called Beautiful" (Acts 3:2).

Although the apostles enjoyed great popularity with the people, opposition from the authorities mounted and eventually broke into open persecution with the stoning of Stephen. This must have dismayed all the believers and resulted in a certain amount of panic. Luke refers in Acts 8 to a large-scale movement out of Jerusalem and to the believers being scattered throughout Judea and Samaria. The record in Acts of the spread of the Gospel indicates that the Church later came to recognise that God actually used the persecution to fulfil his purposes.

Jesus had not only given the Great Commission to go to every part of the world and proclaim the Gospel (Matthew 28:19–20) but he had also given the strategy for fulfilling this mission beginning in Jerusalem where God's act of salvation for the whole of mankind had taken place. "You will be my witnesses in Jerusalem, and in all Judea and Samaria, and to the ends of the earth" (Acts 1:8).

This directive had been preceded (v.4) by the instruction Jesus gave to the disciples to remain in Jerusalem until God had fulfilled his promise to bestow upon them the power of his Spirit that would enable them to fulfil the mission as his witnesses to the whole world. It was God's intention to direct the mission given to his disciples through the Holy Spirit, thus it was essential that from the earliest days they should learn to wait upon him, to listen to him, to trust him completely and to be absolutely obedient. This meant learning to remain still and be quiet as well as knowing when to act and to speak out boldly. The major lesson the believers had to learn before Pentecost was that they were to do nothing on their own initiative but were to act only under the direction, and through the empowering of the Holy Spirit.

The significance of Pentecost is that it inaugurated the "age of the Spirit". It was not just one special day or even a special generation that Peter was referring to when he said that the prophecy of Joel was being fulfilled that day – it was the day of inauguration, the day upon which

God began to carry out the intention he had had since the beginning of creation and to fulfil the vision he had revealed to his servants the prophets over a period of many hundreds of years.

We are emphasising this point here because today we are surrounded by a rising tide of New Age teaching declaring that the Age of the Spirit is about to begin with the dawn of the "Age of Aquarius" around the year AD 2000. New Agers teach that in the world of astronomy a new star comes into ascendancy every 2,100 years bringing in a "new age" by a paradigm shift into its characteristics.

They say that a new age began around the year 2200 BC with Abraham's sacrifice of the ram instead of his son. This was the age of "Aries the Ram". It represented a spiritual shift in the thinking of mankind in relation to the gods who prior to this were primarily thought of as female such as Astarte and Diana. Abraham taught the "Fatherhood of God" and this began the era of male dominance.

The new age that began around the year 100 BC was marked by the birth of Jesus when the Magi saw the new star sign over Bethlehem. New Agers say that this was the age of "Pisces the Fish" and that Jesus acknowledged this by choosing fishermen for his close companions, telling them they would become "fishers of men" and the Early Church adopted the "sign of the fish" as the symbol of Christian faith. New Agers say that this was the "Age of the Son" in contrast to the previous age as the "Age of the Father".

They further say that the next New Age that will begin with the year AD 2000 will be the "Age of Aquarius the Water Bearer" and this will be the "Age of the Spirit". It will mark a new period of spirituality when the Spirit of God will come upon all people. Their expectation is for the coming together of all religions and the releasing

10

within every individual of spiritual forces of creativity that are linked with mother nature as the source of all creative energy. They believe that humankind will be released from the bondage imposed by the concept of sin and guilt so that all people can exercise their true liberty and achieve their divine potentiality and actually become gods.

Clearly this is very different from what Peter foresaw as the fulfilment of Joel's prophecy beginning on the day of Pentecost. The full power of the Holy Spirit was already present with the apostles and new believers. There is no statement anywhere in the New Testament to suggest that the Spirit would be withdrawn at the end of the apostolic age or indeed at any other point in history. The Holy Spirit was given to the Church to enable the carrying out of the mission of Christ which is summarised in the Great Commission.

From the day of Pentecost until today there has been no difference in the power of the Holy Spirit available to believers. The differences have been in *quantity* not in *quality*. As the number of believers throughout the world increases, so the quantity of Holy Spirit being poured out increases, because it is the promise of God to pour out his Spirit upon all believers regardless of worldly distinctions which include distinctions of race and nationality.

It is therefore quite wrong to expect God to give us a greater quality of spiritual power in the last days of the present age than in the earliest days. Jesus' promise "greater things than these will you do" was spoken to his own disciples. We are perfectly correct in saying that this promise applies to us today, but it applies to us *equally* with the believers in the New Testament church and the apostolic age. It is a misinterpretation of scripture to suggest that it applies in some special way to believers in the final generations leading up to the Second Coming of Christ.

11

A New Prophetic End Time Movement?

Those who are speaking of a "new breed" of believers today are not only misinterpreting scripture but are actually giving teaching that is dangerously close to that of the New Age movement. We are most certainly not just entering a "new age of spirituality" wherein men and women will perform supernatural deeds, walking through walls, stretching out their hands with fire flowing from them to strike down opponents of the Gospel. These are just some of the fantastic deeds which are being "prophesied" by some of those who see themselves as part of a new prophetic movement. These exploits owe more to TV "superman" movies than to scripture.

Yes, indeed, there is a new prophetic movement today! And it is the purpose of this book to take note of this new move of the Spirit. But we also need to be aware of the counterfeit, because any new move of God is always accompanied by an attempt by the spiritual forces of darkness to confuse believers. The new prophetic movement *is* one of the signs of the times that we need to note in order to gain a clear understanding of the way God is working out his purposes today. Any study of contemporary events and trends, both secular and in the church, should take note of biblical prophecy if we wish to understand what God is doing today and what the Spirit is saying to the churches.

There are many indications given in the New Testament which enable believers to be aware of what Jesus refers to as "the end of the age". We should beware of being pushed by New Agers into accepting their timetable of events and their interpretation instead of studying scripture and taking note only of what is said in the word of God and how the Spirit of God is interpreting this to us today.

As we draw closer to the end of the second millennium and the dawn of the year 2000 it is not only New Agers who are getting excited. The biblical forecasters also are busy working out their mathematical formulae and predictions of dates and times in direct disobedience to Jesus' instruction in Acts 1:7 "It is not for you to know the times and dates the Father has set by his own authority." Jesus' instruction was to "watch and pray" and to be ready at all times for his coming.

"Watching" most certainly does mean being aware of rapidly changing events in the contemporary world and spreading these before the Lord in prayer for the Holy Spirit to give us understanding. But it does not mean joining the New Agers, the occultists, diviners, spiritists and astrologers in predicting the timetable that the Father had not even revealed to the Son during the period of his earthly ministry, and which he most certainly does not intend to reveal to us.

It is the Father's intention that we should walk by *faith* and not by sight, trusting only in the Lord Jesus, our only Saviour. It is the spirit of the world which wants to know what will happen tomorrow, and drives people to read their horoscopes in the daily papers, and to run after fortune-tellers and astrologers. The Spirit of Jesus, by contrast, bids us be still and know that God is in control.

The world in our generation is full of false prophets and false teachers but we should not be surprised at this for this is one of the signs of the end of the age that Jesus referred to in Matthew 24. It is worth noting that before he gave his list of signs to the disciples, the first thing he said was a solemn warning about deception "Watch out that no one deceives you" (24:4). We need to keep this warning constantly in front of us in seeking to interpret contemporary events.

In order to understand what is happening today and the rise of the "new prophetic movement" we need to see it in the context of the whole move of God during the Twentieth Century. There can be no doubt that the most outstanding feature of this century has been the spread of the worldwide Pentecostal Movement. Most church historians regard the 1906 Azusa Street revival in Los Angeles as the beginning of modern Pentecostalism, but there is evidence of many smaller-scale similar events taking place around that time in different parts of the world. Clearly, God began to pour out his Spirit with abundance in a new way at the beginning of the Twentieth Century.

Church growth statistician David Barrett estimates that there were around three million Pentecostal Spirit-filled believers throughout the world in the year 1900. That represents less than one per cent of the total membership of the church at the beginning of this century. The number of Christians worldwide has tripled since that time from more than 550 million to nearly 1,760 million, about one-third of whom would be Pentecostal/ charismatics.

This phenomenal growth of Spirit-filled believers is one of the major spiritual characteristics of the century and in order to understand its significance as a work of God and a fulfilment of biblical prophecy we need to note where this expansion has taken place.

The facts are that with the expansion of the world population and the even greater percentage growth of the Christian Church, the "centre" of the Christian world has shifted.

At the beginning of the Twentieth Century sixty-five per cent of all Christians were in the western industrialised nations and only seventeen per cent in the "two-thirds-world" but by 1988 the percentages had reversed to thirty-nine per cent and fifty-three per cent.

If this trend continues, by the end of this century the contrast is expected to be even more marked with only thirty-two per cent of Christians being from western nations and almost twice as many, sixty-one per cent from these developing nations.

It is often said that Africa, south of the Sahara, is now the "spiritual centre" of the world with its emphasis upon the power of God. But South–East Asia, which a few years ago was considered one of the most difficult areas of the world for evangelism, is now challenging for this title.

South Korea is well known for the size of its churches – anything under two thousand members is considered small – many are in the hundreds of thousands with the largest having three-quarters-of-a-million. Indonesia, although still officially a Muslim country, has seen continued remarkable growth since the revival started in 1965 when a civil war was at its height. Singapore has been a centre for renewal since 1972 with every Anglican church moving in the things of the Spirit. The growth rate of the church in China has been phenomenal, growing from less than one million believers when the doors to the West were closed by the Communist revolution in 1949, to between fifty and a hundred million today with some areas growing as fast as ten thousand new believers a day.

If we look at the worldwide scene, we can see certain trends running through. For example:

When a nation is persecuted, the people are open to God working; but when a nation feels in control of its own destiny, the people will often reject God.

When a nation is suffering uncertainty and experiencing national upheavals and shakings, the people will turn to God for help; but when a nation is secure, the people become self-sufficient and tend to turn away from God – nominality becomes the norm. Israel constantly fell into this trap. Through Hosea, God said, "When I fed them, they were satisfied; when they were satisfied, they became proud; then they forgot me" (Hosea 13:6).

When a people have few material possessions, their hope is in God; but when they become rich, they forget or reject him. Among the sayings of Agur, we read the prayer "Give me neither poverty nor riches, but give me only my daily bread. Otherwise I may have too much and disown you and say, 'Who is the Lord?' Or I may become poor and steal, and so dishonour the name of my God" (Proverbs 30:8–10).

When a nation is serviced by foreign missionaries, the growth rate will be slow; but when a people takes responsibility for sharing the Gospel themselves, then the growth rate escalates and the Church multiplies.

When a nation puts undue emphasis upon the "individual" instead of the "community", the people become inward-looking and élitist; but when a nation sees itself as having responsibility for others, "belongingness" and *koinonia* (fellowship) are emphasised and concern is shown for others and the church grows.

It is most significant to note that the great outpouring of the Spirit of God in this century, has been mostly upon the poor, the status-less and the persecuted. This surely links with Joel's prophecy that God would pour out his Spirit upon àll people – rich and poor.

In Jesus' first public sermon in Nazareth, he emphasised that the Spirit of the Lord was upon him to preach good news to the poor, to proclaim freedom for the prisoners, recovery of sight for the blind, to release the oppressed, as well as to proclaim the year of the Lord's favour (Luke 4:18–19).

The Gospel turns upside down the values of the world. Jesus continually taught this with such sayings as "Blessed are the meek, for they will inherit the earth" (Matthew 5:5). Paul also saw the radical nature of the

Gospel and he told the Corinthians that "the foolishness of God is wiser than man's wisdom, and the weakness of God is stronger than man's strength" (1 Corinthians 1:25).

"For my thoughts are not your thoughts, neither are your ways my ways, declares the Lord" (Isaiah 55:8). The charismatic movement that has gained momentum worldwide during the second half of the Twentieth Century is a clear illustration of this statement. When God moves in power to fulfil his promises he acts in ways that are different from those of the world and from the expectations of men. It is not the wise, the great and the learned who are first to receive his gifts and to perceive what God is doing, but those who have a childlike trust in God and upon whom the Spirit of the Lord rests in power.

The charismatic renewal has brought two new emphases, particularly to western-style churches:

1) the involvement of ordinary people, and
2) an emphasis upon a personal relationship with God – personal holiness and spirituality.

It has broken all worldly boundaries and has embraced ordinary people while at the same time confounding learned theologians and often bypassing the most powerful leaders of the Church. It has broken across denominational barriers in a way that the cerebral unity movements have been unable to do.

This surely demonstrates the spiritual truth that God is not looking for men's way of doing things through theological commissions, arguments in committee, synod decisions, assembly resolutions and agreed statements of faith. When God moves he simply cuts through the barriers that men think are insurmountable and brings unity among ordinary simple believers who trust Jesus and who care little or nothing for the complexities of ecclesiastical politics. When God does it his way, even the strongholds of church tradition fall silent before him!

The charismatic movement has opened the door to the practice of spiritual gifts, not only in the new fellowships but even in many of the older established churches. Traditional concepts of ministry and priesthood have suppressed the exercise of spiritual gifts among the people for hundreds of years and it is the charismatic revival within the Church that has brought a release from this bondage.

A major part has been played by music which is always a characteristic of revival. The new hymns and songs that have come from charismatic writers and composers have been significant in transforming praise and worship in many churches. They have involved the people in worship as active participants in a new way. The Nineteenth-Century emphasis upon worship led by large choirs and professional organists and singers inevitably led to congregations who were more spectators than performers. Worship today is more in the realm of the DIY than the professional, with the musician who can play by ear being more in demand than the professionally trained expert performer. Praise and worship, in the renewal mode, enables ordinary people to enter into communion with the Lord as they acknowledge the Lordship of Jesus. All believers are able to experience for themselves something of the presence of the Lord.

There are significant indications today that the Pentecostal/charismatic movement is now entering a new prophetic phase. As multitudes of ordinary believers have been brought into communion with the living God, their faith has been transformed from "nominal" to "active". As the experience of believers leads them into a more personal relationship with God, the desire to hear from him grows. Millions of believers are now learning to listen to God as well as to speak to him through prayer. Many groups today spend time in waiting upon the Lord as well as time in intercession. It is this emphasis upon hearing from God, and the desire to learn what he is doing in the world and saying to his people today, that is producing "a new prophetic movement".

Prophecy played a highly important part in the life of the New Testament churches because it was closely related to the right exercise of all the spiritual gifts. Paul makes this clear in his teaching in 1 Corinthians 14 and it is probably for this reason that "prophecy" occurs in all three of his lists of spiritual gifts and ministries (Ephesians 4; 1 Corinthians 12 and Romans 12). It is through prophecy that we hear from God and thereby know how we should be using all the other gifts. Those with prophetic gifts, when rightly practised, act as the eyes and ears of the church and thereby enable the church both to understand the times and to know how to proceed in fulfilling the mission of Christ in the contemporary world.

It is clearly God's intention in the last days to fulfil the wish of Moses that all the people should receive his Spirit and be able to prophesy – to hear from him and to declare his word. God has promised throughout scripture to raise a prophetic people who would be like the tribe of Issachar in the time of King David – they understood the times and knew what Israel should do (1 Chronicles 12:32). God is wanting a listening and an obedient people through whom he can carry out his purposes in these times. He has promised to mobilise his Church into an army of the Lord for the special task demanded of believers at the end of the age. Paul refers to this in Ephesians 3:10 where he speaks of God using the Church to reveal his manifest wisdom and make it "known to the rulers and authorities in the heavenly realms".

It is in order to prepare the Church for these days that the spiritual gifts are being given to all believers through a fresh outpouring of the Holy Spirit today so that each one is rightly equipped. The gifts are given for a purpose, not to be played with in spiritual games like trivial pursuits. When the spiritual gifts are all being rightly exercised in perfect harmony and in love and unity within the church, God is able, not only to reveal his purposes, but also to work them out through an obedient people who are under his authority and directed by the Holy Spirit.

God's purpose in pouring out the Holy Spirit from the beginning of this present age, as Jesus told his disciples, was to evangelise the world. It is the desire of the Father's heart that no one should be lost (1 Timothy 2:4) and therefore he wants the good news of salvation through Jesus to reach people of all nations so that all may have the opportunity of receiving or rejecting Christ before his Second Coming at the end of the age.

In the following chapters we will be examining the evidence for this new prophetic movement. We will look at the way God is revealing his purposes to us today, how he is speaking personally and working in power. We will also take note of the warnings of Jesus about deception and false prophets and the teaching of the New Testament on discernment. Throughout our study we shall be constantly referring to scripture as the plumb line of God's truth.

Chapter Two

The God Who Reveals His Purposes

Why is it that prophecy is catching the attention of so many Christians today? We have already noted that the rise of a new prophetic movement is a characteristic of this present age and that it is also one of the signs of the end of the age that we may expect to see. But what is the significance of prophecy coming to occupy a more prominent place in the life of the church today? If this movement is truly of God we need to ask the fundamental question as to why God is speaking to us prophetically at this particular time.

God Reveals Himself

In order to answer this, we have to turn back to scripture and see the significance of prophecy in the life of a nation that was in a covenant relationship with God. Then we can begin to understand why God is speaking to the Church – the people of the New Covenant – today. The prophets of Israel acted as "the eyes and ears of the nation". They were watchmen for the Lord whose task was to watch for any signs of danger so that they could warn the nation. But they also had to discern what the Lord was doing and to interpret his word to the people.

Amos 3:7 tells us that "the sovereign Lord does nothing without revealing his plan to his servants the prophets". From the beginning of the history of Israel, God chose to use certain individuals to speak to the nation. In the same way as each generation builds upon the accumulated knowledge of previous generations, so in terms of spiritual maturity each generation should be able to build upon the spiritual truths revealed by God to previous generations.

Of course, we each have to find God for ourselves, but God used the prophets of Israel to reveal different aspects of his nature and purposes. This is why we find a different emphasis in each of the great writing prophets in the Bible; one stressing his love, another his mercy, another his justice, but all of them emphasising his faithfulness and his unchanging nature. He was a God who kept his promises and never forsook those with whom he entered a covenant relationship. Today we have the revelation of the Fatherhood of God through the Lord Jesus in addition to all the knowledge of God given to us through the prophets of the Old Covenant to enable us to have a fuller knowledge of the nature and purposes of God.

Throughout the Bible, God is shown to be a God who communicates. Divine truth is revealed to men and women through visions, dreams and the spoken word. These three means of communication are referred to in Numbers 12 when God was rebuking Aaron and Miriam for their attitude towards Moses. "When a prophet of the Lord is among you, I reveal myself to him in visions, I speak to him in dreams. But this is not true of my servant Moses; he is faithful in all my house. With him I speak face to face, clearly and not in riddles; he sees the form of the Lord" (12:6–8).

A further way in which God has always spoken to his servants is through his actions, what the prophets used to refer to as "the deeds of the Lord". Hence Jeremiah spoke of the Lord withholding the spring rains as a sign of his anger with Judah because of their idolatry (usually referred to as [spiritual] "prostitution") (Jeremiah 3:3) and Amos reeled off a catalogue of catastrophes which God had allowed to come upon the nation, each of which was followed by the refrain "yet you have not returned to me, declares the Lord" (Amos 4:6–12).

This illustrates another basic task of prophecy, to interpret the signs of the times and the contemporary deeds of the Lord in such a way that they can be understood even by those who have not learned to get into the presence of the Lord and to know God for themselves. It is God's desire that *all* his people should understand his ways and his purposes and that they should be able to explain to others what he is doing in the world today. For this reason God reveals his truth to believers so that they can communicate it to others. Divine revelation is thus to believers first and then to unbelievers, just as the Gospel was communicated to the Jew first and then to the Gentile (Romans 1:16). Thus in the New Testament, and in the Church today, prophecy is always to the Church. It is for the Church to declare the word of God to the nations. That is the purpose of prophecy. God speaks to his servants, not simply for their own edification but to enable them to declare the Gospel to the world with prophetic power and insight, and thereby to fulfil the Great Commission. The significance of the new prophetic movement today can only be realised when we understand the true purpose of prophecy as declaring the contemporary word of the contemporary God to the contemporary world.

In times of crisis, God always raised up prophets in Israel through whom he communicated his truth to the nation. In New Testament times, the Holy Spirit was given to all believers to enable them to hear from God and to prophesy within the local church situation. They were able to receive divine guidance for the church and for the task of declaring the word of God to unbelievers (1 Corinthians 14:24). Nevertheless, there were also certain individuals known as prophets. These were those who had received what Paul described as the ministry-gift of prophecy (Ephesians 4:11) and were regularly used for the wider ministry of prophecy to the whole church. Their task was to interpret the word of God to the churches in an itinerant ministry such as that exercised by Agabus, Judas and Silas.

The contrast between those who exercised the gift of prophecy (or, more correctly, those who regularly received a manifestation of the Spirit of God in prophecy) in the local church and the prophets whose ministry was exercised among all the churches, is seen in Luke's account of events in Caesarea when Paul was on his way to Jerusalem. He refers to Philip the evangelist who had "four unmarried daughters who had the gift of prophecy" and also to "a prophet named Agabus" who came down from Judea (Acts 21:8–10).

The whole of the Bible bears witness to the nature of God being unchangeable. Today God is still the God who communicates with his people, and if we are right in judging that the present day is a critical period in world history, we must expect God to be speaking.

Accomplishing God's Purposes

When God speaks it is for a particular reason. His word always accomplishes his purpose. He does not give divine revelation simply to provide his people with supernatural knowledge beyond that possessed by the unbelievers. In Isaiah 55, God says that the word that goes out from his mouth "will not return to me empty, but will *accomplish* what I desire and *achieve the purpose* for which I sent it" (v.11). This is one of the tests of genuine prophecy.

Today there are many people who are hearing words

from the Lord concerning the Church and the state of the nations. This is an indication that God is teaching his people to understand the times in which we live and raising the awareness of his people to the significance of these days. He does not expect them all to become itinerant prophets, but rather to seize every opportunity to declare his word to the Church, and to unbelievers as a witness to the world. If, however, a word is received that is both specific and directive, there must be the ability to do something about it if the word is genuinely from the Holy Spirit. God does not give a word that cannot be fulfilled. This is, in fact, one of the tests of this type of prophecy. If it is truly a word from God, even if it seems impossible, he will open the way and give the power to fulfil it.

In 1982 God spoke to me giving me a direct word that I was to call together those who were exercising prophetic ministries in many nations. They would come from every region of the world. The purpose was to share with each other what we were hearing from the Holy Spirit in our own nations and collectively to wait upon the Lord. He said he would reveal his word for these times concerning the nations.

This seemed an utterly impossible task at the time because I had only recently begun to exercise an international ministry and I knew very few people outside Europe. The word was shared with those around us in London and all affirmed it to be a word from the Lord. The next step was to share it with one or two international leaders who visited Britain from time to time. They also affirmed it and they shared it with others so that gradually the word spread. A small international leadership team was formed to take responsibility for the gathering and step by step, what at first had seemed to be highly improbable, began to become a reality.

The leadership group did not actually invite anyone to the meeting; they simply made the prophecy known and it was passed from one to another through many nations. The group believed that it was the Lord who had to do the inviting because he was calling his servants together. Those whom he wanted to be there would hear from him and would respond. The leadership group did, however, take steps to ensure that those who responded were, in fact, known to be exercising prophetic ministries recognised by the churches in their own country.

The international gathering of those with prophetic ministries took place in 1986 after four years of testing and preparation. One hundred and fifty-three leaders and intercessors representing every region of the world gathered on Mount Carmel in Israel for six days of sharing, prayer and waiting upon the Lord.

Even the place where we met had prophetic significance. It was not a hotel and had never been used for a conference nor for anything Christian. It was a rehabilitation centre for survivors of the holocaust built with money from the German Government as part of its reparations to Israel after World War II. When we discovered it in 1984 it was more than forty years after the end of the war and most of the survivors were quite elderly and were becoming fewer in number. The centre had many unused bedrooms and those responsible for it were open to a new role at the time when the Lord led us there as we went from place to place seeking the right venue.

During our times of worship, many of the elderly survivors came to join in the praise, attracted by the music and by the openness and love shown to them. For many of them it was their first personal encounter with Christians since the days of the Nazis, and during the week two of them came to acknowledge Christ as Saviour. Each had an experience of Jesus appearing to them during the night, and each separately sought members of the gathering to ask what this could mean. Each was led to the Lord by Messianic Jews from churches in Israel.

Towards the end of the week, following the times of sharing, the Lord spoke. The prophecy we received said that God was shaking the nations which would intensify and affect the social, political and economic affairs of all nations. The whole natural creation was being shaken and God's intention was to use this period of instability that was coming upon the world to cause mankind to lose confidence in the things of the flesh. It would also break the powers of secular humanism and open up the nations to the Gospel. This would be linked to a period of great spiritual awakening and harvest throughout the world. There was a clear witness in the whole gathering that this was indeed the word of the Lord for our times.

The scriptures received by the gathering that confirmed these promises centred around the prophecy of Haggai 2:6 and 7. "This is what the Lord Almighty says: 'In a little while I will once more shake the heavens and the earth, the sea and the dry land. I will shake all nations, and the desired of all nations will come, and I will fill this house with glory', says the Lord Almighty."

This prophecy is repeated in Hebrews 12:26f, which shows that it was still unfulfilled in New Testament times, and an interpretation is given which refers to the time of shaking as being when God would establish his kingdom.

There was a common witness in the gathering that this prophecy was beginning to be fulfilled in our generation. God is preparing the way by speaking to those with prophetic insight so that they can understand the way he is working out his purposes and the response he is requiring from his people. This is a day of preparation which God is using to train his people, and that is why we are seeing evidence of a fresh outpouring of the Holy

Spirit, and spiritual gifts being widely distributed among believers throughout the world.

When God speaks to us prophetically with a direct word, he also gives the strategy for its fulfilment, just as he did when he gave the seemingly impossible task of world evangelisation to the disciples, that we know as the Great Commission. Jesus gave them the overall strategy plus the promise that the Holy Spirit would be with them to guide them in the day-to-day detail. God follows the same method today and it is important for the Church to know this, not just in theory but in practice, and therefore to be able to trust the Father completely to fulfil his promise and to know that if he sets his servants a task he will give the ability to fulfil it. Paul knew this as he had many times seen God carry out seemingly impossible tasks throughout his missionary activities. He told the believers in Ephesus that God "is able to do immeasurably more than all we ask or imagine, according to his power that is at work within us" (Ephesians 3:20).

The Lord taught us this lesson many times during our ministry in the East End of London so that we learnt to trust him in all circumstances – in times of hardship as well as in times when the ministry was flourishing. In fact it was during the hard times that we learnt to trust him most and we came to see this as a preparation for the times of greater responsibility in international ministry. God actually puts us through times of stern testing before entrusting us with major responsibilities. This surely is the meaning of Jesus' parable of the talents and the stewards who were given minor responsibilities before being trusted to handle greater things (Matthew 25:14–30). This is not just to give us wider experience of his ways but to increase our confidence in him, our recognition that we can do nothing on our own, and our absolute trust in his ability to carry out his promises and to fulfil his word.

It was this confidence in God that enabled me to stand on the word I received during the time of preparation for the Carmel gathering. In 1984 four of us went to Israel to seek the place of the Lord's appointing for the prophetic gathering and to make arrangements for a large international congress in Jerusalem where the word of the Lord would be declared publicly. We ended our two weeks in Israel by staying at the Jerusalem Towers Hotel not far from the Jaffa Gate entrance to the Old City. Two days before we were due to return to Britain, the Lord woke me early in the morning with the words, "Danger! Beware Monday 16th April". It was about 3 a.m. on Friday 13th April. My first thoughts were for our children back home in England but as I prayed for further understanding, it was made clear that this was nothing to do with our family. I woke Monica and we prayed together for a while and then decided to go up onto the Mount of Olives to pray. The Old City was still in darkness as we made our way around the walls and up the slope where Jesus and the disciples had often climbed, to a place where we thought we would be undisturbed while the new day dawned over Jerusalem.

I sought the Lord urgently for revelation. Was it God who had woken me? Were the words I had heard simply my own imagination or was God really saying something significant to me? If so, what was the meaning? During this time of intercession, the Lord again spoke and said "It is not your family who are in danger, but the nation Israel. I have brought you here to hear my word. There will be an attack launched against Israel by Syria on Monday 16th April and you must warn the nation." I shared this with Monica and together we prayed to know what should be done. Many questions ran through our minds. Why would the Lord give such a message to two strangers on their first visit to the Middle East who knew hardly anyone in Israel and who had no dealings with anyone in authority and apparently no ability to do anything about the word? But we knew that God never gives a wasted word, so either it was not genuinely from God or there was something further that we had to do.

We returned to the hotel and shared the word with another minister and his wife who had accompanied us on this trip to Israel. The four of us had a time of intercession asking the Lord to confirm the word if it was truly from him and to show us what he required us to do. It was during this time we remembered that we were due to go to the home of Lance Lambert that evening for a Shabbat meal with his family. We concluded that God was telling us to share the word with Lance after the meal and to seek his advice.

We had known Lance Lambert when he was pastor of a church in Richmond, London, before he discovered his Jewish roots and received a word from the Lord directing him to settle in Israel. At that time we knew nothing of his family background or of how his father, a member of the Italian aristocracy, had died in Auschwitz whilst he was still an infant and how his mother had escaped to England with Lance and his sister. Neither did we know anything of his access to members of the Israeli government.

When the Shabbat meal was finished I described the events of that morning with the exact words which I believed I had heard from the Lord and we all prayed together. We discussed the possibility of an attack from Syria, and recognised that Monday 16th April would an ideal time for a surprise attack against Israel because it was the first day of the Jewish Passover. Lance, nevertheless, said that he thought it was highly unlikely because there was no special alert and Israeli military intelligence was usually highly efficient.

It was after midnight before we went back to the hotel and we received no further word from Lance during the next thirty-six hours before our flight back to London. On Monday 16th we listened to every news bulletin but there was no word of any attack against Israel or any hint of an escalation in the tensions of the Middle East. Nothing happened the next day or the next and the whole Passover week slipped by without incident. We concluded that the word could not have been from the Lord but that at least we had been faithful in following through and testing what we thought God was saying. We put the whole episode out of our minds and returned to normal ministry matters.

One month later Lance Lambert came to London and telephoned asking me to meet him. He sounded excited and I arranged to go the next day. This was the remarkable story he had to tell –

Early on the Saturday morning, Lance began telephoning a few trusted Christian leaders in Jerusalem and shared with them the word I had received asking them to pray about it and call him back. By mid-morning most had rung to say that they had no specific word from the Lord but that they felt the word should be taken seriously. They all said "We know Clifford Hill exercises a prophetic ministry, and a warning such as this should not be ignored". This confirmed Lance's own assessment. He immediately called a Government Minister who was a near neighbour and passed on to him the words of warning, saying they came from a Christian preacher whom he knew to be trustworthy. The Minister reacted dismissively saying there could be no truth in the suggestion of an impending attack from Syria or he would certainly have been aware of it. He nevertheless promised to take it seriously and at least check with his military advisors.

Two hours later the Minister came to Lance's house and began asking him numerous questions about his informant. Who did I work for? What were the details of my academic background? What were my political affiliations? Did I have specific connections with Syria? Lance answered all these questions to the best of his ability saying that I was an ordained clergyman, that this was my first visit to the Middle East and that as far as he knew I certainly had no political connections in the area. The Minister was convinced that I must have high level contacts in Syria and he told Lance that they had spy satellite information showing the movement of Syrian forces massing in southern Syria and moving towards the Golan Heights. They appeared to be poised for an invasion of Southern Lebanon and Northern Israel.

Within hours Israel went onto Number One Alert. Throughout the weekend reserves were mobilised and the whole nation quietly went onto a full war footing in preparation for the expected attack. Lance called a meeting of Christian leaders in his home on the Sunday afternoon to discuss the situation. They concluded that the Lord had revealed the plans of the enemy for one of two reasons; either to enable Israel's defences to be mobilised in time to resist an attack or because he wished the Messianic believers in the nation to do something about it and that he would use the situation for a witness to the leaders. They decided that in any case they had better start praying. They began a time of fervent intercession for the peace of Jerusalem and for the protection of Israel.

By six o'clock that evening a storm swept across the land and struck Jerusalem with hurricane-force winds and torrential rain. Lance said the noise of the storm was at times so great that they could not hear each other pray. They were shouting above the tumult outside. Several times he opened his eyes and looked at the window expecting to see a tree in the yard outside come crashing through. The storm lasted all night and right through the day of Monday 16th April and through to Tuesday 17th. It covered the whole of Israel, Southern Lebanon, Southern Syria and Eastern Jordan.

On Wednesday 18th, Lance met the Minister who quietly said, "Lance, the storm saved us". He reported that they had information indicating the invasion was to have begun with a missile attack followed by a full-scale assault by tanks and troops, but the ground was so soft that the heavy armoured vehicles would not have been able to make any progress. Once the surprise element had been lost, the planned assault had been cancelled. He also told Lance that the Israeli Intelligence had been checking out his friend. "So far", he said, "we have been unable to locate Clifford Hill's source of information." Lance hoped they would soon do so!

When this incident occurred it was a particularly dangerous time for Israel, with considerable tensions in the Middle East. It was only a few months after the bombing of the American Embassy in Beirut and the withdrawal of Western forces from Lebanon. Syria had large forces in Lebanon and was making warlike noises of what would happen if there were an attempt from the West to interfere. It was widely interpreted that Syria was seeking to become the dominant power in the Middle East and she was being supplied with large quantities of sophisticated arms from the Soviet Union. Following the American and French withdrawal from Lebanon there was a power gap in the area. A surprise attack during the Feast of the Passover would have been the ideal opportunity for Syria to take advantage of the situation and to achieve what all the Muslim/Arab neighbours of Israel have sought since 1948 – the destruction of Israel.

It should be apparent to all except the most rabid anti-semitist, that God has been watching over Israel since the formation of the modern State by a resolution of the United Nations that was even supported by the Soviet Union. This in itself was seen by many to be a miraculous birth similar to the reference in Isaiah 66:8 "Who has ever heard of such a thing? Who has seen such things? Can a country be born in a day or a nation be brought forth in a moment?" This prophecy concerning the rebirth of the nation also contains the promise "I will extend peace to her like a river" (v.12) and although that peace has not yet been seen in an absence of hostilities, it certainly has been seen in the protection of the nation despite numerous threats, wars and assaults that probably no other nation in the world could have survived.

God's protection over Israel does not mean that the whole nation is in a state of spiritual righteousness in the eyes of God – far from it. Modern Israel is one of the most secular nations in the world, with the majority of its population not even believing in God even though the Sabbath and the feasts and festivals are regularly observed. Most of the kibbutzim were formed on an atheistic basis with no synagogue, no recognition of the Law, but teaching a Marxist philosophy. Clearly God has had a purpose in replanting the nation in the land, but until there is full acknowledgement of God, the nation must be in danger. If Jeremiah were in Jerusalem today he would be thundering warnings that God, who is holy and righteous, will not protect an unholy and unrighteous nation. There is a limit to his patience.

But remarkable things are happening in Israel today as more and more Jews acknowledge Jesus as their Messiah. Many of them are shy of calling themselves "Christians" because of the centuries of persecution they have endured at the hands of Gentiles who claimed to be acting as Christians. Most of the believers in Israel today prefer the term "Messianic". Since 1985 there has been a remarkable growth of Messianic fellowships and most recently the inflow of immigrants from the USSR has boosted this number. Many of the newcomers were already believers or were open to the Gospel having had no orthodox Jewish teaching which was banned in Communist Russia.

The most remarkable feature of the growing number of Israeli citizens who have become Messianic believers is that many of them did not come to faith through evangelism but through a personal encounter with the Lord Jesus. In 1989, Messianic leaders were saying that roughly half of all the believers in Israel could bear witness to having received a personal revelation of Jesus that brought them to faith. We have also heard of many Jews in other parts of the world coming to Christ in the same way. The first record of a Jew coming to faith in this way was, of course, the conversion of Paul (Acts 8). We know of no other people groups among whom this is happening today. Clearly God has a special purpose to fulfil in his dealings with the descendants of those with whom he first entered a covenant relationship in the time of Abraham, and promised "all nations on earth will be blessed through him" (Genesis 18:18).

If we are right in believing that we are already seeing signs that we are nearing the end of the age, then we should expect to begin to see the fulfilment of the promises of God that were given to the Jews, including the promise of Romans 11 that all Israel will be saved. Paul says that "they are loved on account of the patriarchs, for God's gifts and his call are irrevocable" (vv.28–29). Paul's vision throughout his writings was that the day would come when the dividing wall of hostility between Jew and Gentile would be broken down and they would become one in Christ and "members of God's household, built on the foundation of the apostles and prophets, with Christ Jesus himself as the chief cornerstone" (Ephesians 2:19–20).

Paul used the illustration of an olive tree in Romans 11. He prophesies that the day will come when Israel will be grafted back into the olive tree and thus take her place alongside gentile believers within the household of God. This gives a picture of what we may expect to see. Today God is beginning to fulfil his promises and he is doing so in his own way. It is for this reason that we are seeing more activity of God in revelation but, as we have already noted, when God acts in divine revelation it is always for a purpose.

Handling Revelation

When the word was received about the danger of an attack from Syria, we knew that if it were a genuine word from God there would be something that could be done about it and that God would also reveal how the word was to be handled. We, ourselves, have not always acted rightly in responding to divine revelation, and we believe there are many lessons that the church needs to learn in handling contemporary words from God.

There are many thousands of churches today where prophecy is being exercised and prophetic words are being received which are simply ignored. Very often this is not because the leadership do not believe in the spiritual gifts but because they do not know how to handle prophecy. We have often been to churches where during a time of worship prophetic words are spoken but they are neither tested nor seriously considered. Often the leader will simply say "Thank you Jesus" and hurry on to the next song. This is directly contrary to the teaching of the New Testament which instructs us to weigh all prophecy. When prophecy is treated in this way it is, in fact, despised, which again is contrary to Paul's instruction in 1 Thessalonians 5:20.

If God is in fact saying something to the church, then we ought to listen; if it is not from him we should have the courage to say so because Jesus also exhorted his disciples to guard the sheep. This particularly applies to leaders who have the responsibility for guarding the church against deception. The Holy Spirit, according to Jesus' teaching, is "the Spirit of truth". God will not mislead his people but we have to learn to distinguish between truth and error and to discern clearly what the Spirit is saying to the churches today.

This lays upon leadership a heavy responsibility for knowing the word of God revealed to us in scripture, and thereby being familiar with the declared purposes of God. This will enable us, as we observe what is happening in the contemporary world, to discern how God is fulfilling his promises today. This gives us a solid scriptural foundation for weighing prophecy. The witness of the Holy Spirit within us enables us to perceive whether or not the words we are hearing are in accordance with the declared purposes of God in scripture and with the deeds of the Lord today. Weighing prophecy is not nearly so difficult as it sounds. Every leader should have the ability to do this basic testing of the kind of words that are received in the churches simply by asking the questions: Does it accord with scripture? Is this in line with what God is doing today? Does this word breathe the Spirit of the living God? Is it spoken in love? Does it build up the faith and the vision of the body?

In the team with whom we work we have made many mistakes, even though a major part of our ministry is to teach others how to handle divine revelation, how to listen to God and how to test what we are hearing. On one occasion in 1987 we were teaching a leadership seminar as part of a five-day mission on the theme "The Word of God for our Times".

We were in the city of Sheffield and as we were driving to the final morning meeting we passed the Football Ground, and as we did so one of the Team, Edmund Heddle, said he was receiving a picture of a dramatic event that God was revealing to him. We stopped the car at that point to allow him to describe what he was seeing. We recognised that God was speaking to Edmund and we received it as a word from the Lord. It was revealed to him that there would be a tragedy involving loss of life and a major crowd disturbance during a football match in this city. We took this word to the meeting and shared it with the eighty or so leaders (mostly local clergy and ministers) when Edmund advised that they should seek the Lord for further guidance. It was briefly prayed over during the time of intercession that morning but nothing further was done about it.

Two years later this word was tragically fulfilled in one of the worst football crowd disasters ever known in Britain where ninety-five Liverpool supporters, many of them children, were crushed to death on the crowd barriers when the ground became overfull during an FA Cup match between Liverpool and Nottingham Forest at the Sheffield Hillsborough ground. A number of the Sheffield ministers contacted us after this terrible event recalling the revelation we had received and regretting that they had done nothing about it. We, ourselves, felt convicted that we did not take the warning sufficiently seriously and seek the Lord for an understanding of why he had given advance warning of this event and what he intended us to do with it.

Revelation is always given for a purpose. God's word

does not return to him without accomplishing that purpose. If we do not rightly handle the word that is given to us we are accountable to the Lord. There is no ministry more demanding than the prophetic ministry or one that carries greater responsibility. We simply do not know whether the tragic events at the Hillsborough Stadium could have been prevented if we had sought the Lord for an understanding of what he was requiring of us. If we had sought further clarification the Lord may have wanted to reveal to us the danger that existed through the caging in of spectators with no means of escape onto the pitch when the crush of the crowd behind became intolerable. If we had received this further revelation, the local church leaders could then have conveyed it to the football authorities in the city and the human tragedy involving so many families might have been prevented. Such is the responsibility of the right handling of prophecy and the prophetic ministry.

There are many other ways in which prophetic revelation can be mishandled. For example, it is a grave temptation for those who receive prophecy to use it to gain their own ends or even to further the development of their ministry. Often this is done by adding to words received or through the misinterpretation of prophetic pictures or a divinely revealed vision. We love to put our own interpretation upon a word in order to make it fit our own preconceived ideas. This is the commonest fault in prophecy. Many people begin speaking with a word which they are rightly hearing from God and then add to it either because they don't know when to stop or because of a lack of spiritual discipline that allows the flesh to get in. This kind of situation requires sensitive leadership if it is to be rightly handled. When the leadership acts firmly but in love, correction is given that enables the whole body to mature. The one bringing the word will not feel crushed or rejected, but will have learned a lesson in discernment and spiritual discipline.

A further way in which prophecy can be mishandled is through manipulation. Early in 1990 the Kansas City Fellowship (KCF) acknowledged a number of errors in their teaching and practice, particularly in regard to the handling of prophecy. One of these "errors" was in the use of "prophetic gifting for controlling purposes".

An example of this kind of thing occurred in 1989 when Bob Jones, one of those exercising a prophetic ministry in KCF, reported that he had received in a vision a picture of a church that would join the Kansas City Fellowship. He described the building and the exact location of an Assemblies of God Church in Kansas City. Word of this quickly spread, and in due time most of the congregation together with its pastor voted to leave their denomination and link with KCF. This, of course, created resentment within the Assemblies of God and among other churches in Kansas City and left KCF open to the charge of manipulation.

There is no way now of knowing whether or not the original vision and prophecy were genuine. The only way to have tested such a word would have been if the leadership had maintained strict secrecy and waited to see whether it was fulfilled. By letting it become widely known in the city, KCF opened themselves to the charge of misusing prophecy to influence the behaviour of others in order to increase their church membership. Those members of the AOG who believed the prophecy may have been influenced in their thinking and actions in a way that would not have occurred if they had not known of it. Additionally, those who did not believe the prophecy may have been put under pressure for their unbelief. Many churches have been torn asunder by division in this way where one half of the fellowship accept a prophecy as being a true word from God and the others do not. This can be particularly devastating where the prophecy is directive and concerns a whole fellowship. There have been many instances of this kind of manipulative prophecy being used to take over churches in Britain, as well as the USA, during the past twenty years.

Clearly prophecy can be misused, as a means of controlling the lives of others by claiming divine authority for a word or vision that indicates or directs a particular line of action. This is one of the marks of counterfeit revelation of which Christians need to be aware and against which they should be constantly on guard. The counterfeit can often be extremely subtle due to the convincing nature of the revelation and the outward spiritual holiness with which it is surrounded.

This is one of the charges brought by those who fear that the apparitions of Mary at Medjugorje in Yugoslavia are not genuinely divine revelation. This is not the place to make major pronouncements concerning the truth or falsity of the thousands of reported appearances of Mary that have been occurring all over the world in increasing numbers throughout this century. Whether or not they are regarded as genuine is probably largely determined by whether one is Catholic or Protestant since they represent fundamentally different attitudes towards Mary, the mother of Jesus.

There are, however, three major sets of biblical principles that apply to all divine revelation. The first is in regard to the *source* of the revelation, the second is in regard to the *message* and the third is in regard to the *fruit*.

The First Letter of John makes it clear that there are three main sources of spiritual revelation – the human spirit, the Holy Spirit and evil spirits. Only the Holy Spirit can convey divine truth. All other sources of revelation are either demonically inspired or simply figments of the imagination. That which comes from the human spirit may simply be misleading but that which comes from demonic sources is dangerous counterfeit. There can, of course, be various combinations of these sources. Those who constantly indulge in fantasies of the mind may leave the door open to demonic influences and even those who are genuinely receiving a word from the Holy Spirit may drift off into the flesh.

Sometimes an evil spirit can speak the truth which can cause considerable confusion unless there are those able to exercise spiritual discernment and to deal firmly with the matter. A good example of this is reported in Acts 16:16f where Paul and Silas in Philippi were followed by a fortune-telling "slave girl who had a spirit by which she predicted the future". She followed the apostles for several days shouting "These men are servants of the Most High God, who are telling you the way to be saved". There was nothing wrong with the message, but eventually Paul became increasingly troubled because he knew that the source of her spiritual channelling was evil, so he turned around and rebuked the spirit, "In the name of Jesus Christ I command you to come out of her!" and she was immediately delivered.

The thing that troubles many Protestants in regard to the apparitions of Mary is that she is not God, and the witness of scripture is that it is only the Holy Spirit who can convey divine truth; there is no other genuine source of revelation. Either it comes from the Holy Spirit or it is not from God – that is the dilemma. Catholics, on the other hand, are quite used to the concept of prayer to Mary and the saints. An extreme Protestant view of this is that it is necromancy – communicating with the spirits of the departed. A leading Catholic charismatic said recently that although he did not believe the apparitions of Mary to be genuine, he did believe there was evidence that they were being used to convey divine revelation. He said that God is speaking to us today, and if the only way he can get through to Catholics is through their belief in Mary, then he would do so but it was his belief that the revelations were not really from Mary but from the Holy Spirit.

Any message that comes from God is conveyed to us through the Holy Spirit. This is the teaching of Jesus in John's Gospel and it is the witness of the apostles throughout the New Testament. Jesus said "When he, the Spirit of truth comes, he will guide you into all truth. He will not speak on his own; he will speak only what he hears, and he will tell you what is yet to come" (John 16:13). Nowhere in the New Testament is there any suggestion that God would communicate with us through Mary, or through anyone else or any channel other than directly through the Holy Spirit.

Quite apart from the problem of the source of revelation, there is the separate issue of the messages themselves. All messages that purport to be of divine origin must be regarded as prophecy and the New Testament gives clear guidelines for weighing prophecy. A major test is whether or not the word received conforms to the Bible as the established word of God. If in any way it contradicts scripture it cannot be of God because God cannot contradict himself. The messages received at Medjugorje or anywhere else should be weighed in this way.

Some of the reported messages given by Mary at Medjugorje appear to be contrary to scripture, for example: "You are mine, little children. I love you and want you to entrust yourselves to me, thus enabling me to lead you to God. . . . Pray that you may come to realise that you are mine" (25th May 1988), and similarly "Dear children! Today I again invite each one of you to make an option in favour of complete abandonment to me. Only thus will I, in turn, be enabled to offer you to God. You are aware, dear children, that I love you immensely and want each one of you to belong to me" (25th November 1987). These statements appear to be attempting to draw believers into an intimate relationship with Mary rather than with Jesus.

Paul warned us against those who would try to ensnare us into other loyalties "It is for freedom that Christ has set us free. Stand firm, then, and do not let yourselves be burdened again by a yoke of slavery" (Galatians 5:1). In the Old Testament any attempt by a prophet to turn the people's loyalty away from God was regarded as "rebellion against the Lord" (Deuteronomy 13:5) which was punishable by death.

The messages of Mary at Medjugorje even claim to be able to present us sinless to God, "I invite you to give yourself up to me so that I can offer you to God, fresh and without sin. Satan has taken over part of my plan and wants to make it his own. Pray that he may not succeed, because I want you for myself so that I might offer you to God. Thank you for responding to my call!" (1st August 1985). But the New Testament declares that it is only the blood of Jesus that purifies us from all sin (1 John 1:7). It is only Jesus who can present us sinless before the Father (Jude 24). Even the Pharisees recognised that only God can forgive sins (Luke 5:21). Thus to ascribe to Mary the ability to cleanse us from sin is either to deny the uniqueness of Christ's work of redemption upon the cross, or to ascribe divinity to Mary.

There are many other statements in the messages given at Medjugorje that appear to be contrary to scripture. For example, on 28th December 1987, Mary was reported to have said "Wherever I go, and my son is always with me, Satan comes after me". This statement implies that Jesus is continually following Mary around the world and they are both constantly harassed by Satan. The New Testament, by contrast, speaks of Jesus as "having disarmed the powers and authorities, he made a public spectacle of them, triumphing over them by the cross" and that having won the victory over Satan he is now "seated at the right hand of God" (Colossians 2:15, 3:1). There is certainly nothing in the New Testament to indicate that Jesus is still being pursued by Satan.

Another example of a message appearing to contradict scripture is Mary's reported statement of 25 February 1988 "I ask for your prayers. Offer them to me for those who are under Satan's power so that they may be saved. Be a witness through your life. Sacrifice your life for the salvation of the world. I am with you and wish to thank you." Jesus' own teaching on the subject of salvation was that "God so loved the world that he gave his one and only Son, that whoever believes in him should not perish but have eternal life" (John 3:16). The teaching of the apostles, which became the basis of faith throughout the Church, was stated by Peter when he faced the Sanhedrin "Salvation is found in no one else, for there is no other name under heaven given to men by which we must be saved" (Acts 4:12). No amount of human sacrifice can avail for the salvation of the world. New Testament Christianity is perfectly clear that Jesus Christ alone is our Saviour.

The major criticism which Catholic renewal leaders have of the messages at Medjugorje is that they reflect a legalistic tradition that is far from renewal with a strong emphasis upon the repetition of formal prayers and with specific instructions on fasting. No doubt this reflects the kind of spirituality the young people receiving the messages have been taught, but renewal leaders believe it is not what the Holy Spirit is saying today.

In judging the validity of the appearances of Mary, consideration also has to be given to the thousands of testimonies of those whose lives have been changed by a visit to Medjugorje. Numerous books, magazine articles and television programmes have focused on the response of the millions who have gone to Yugoslavia since the appearances began to be reported in 1981. Many of the life-changing experiences have been among those who were neither Catholics nor believers. Those who deny the genuineness of the appearances of Mary have either to say that these conversions represent delusions, or are the work of a counterfeit spirit. The question then arises as to whether God can bring someone to a genuine conversion experience despite the activity of demonic spirits. If the fruit of a ministry is good, does that mean that the ministry is of God? Jesus certainly spoke of fruit as being an important factor in judging a ministry "by their fruit you will recognise them" (Matthew 7:20). But he was referring to people, not apparitions of the dead, however holy they may have been during their lifetime.

But fruit is not only seen in the *immediate* effect upon people's lives which may, or may not, be lasting and which may, or may not, lead them into the truth. Fruit is to be seen in the genuineness of the messages themselves, and whether they lead people into a true and lasting knowledge of God which in turn bears good fruit in their lives. It is here that we need to stress again the importance of testing all divine revelation at the bar of scripture.

If it is true that God is using Mary to speak to Catholics today, because of the centuries of Catholic veneration of her as the mother of our Lord, her messages cannot be regarded as being more accurate than those conveyed by the Holy Spirit. They must surely be tested in the same way. If indeed they are from God, then they must conform to the unchanging word of God already declared in scripture because God cannot contradict himself.

All prophecy is conveyed through human beings and through the imperfect medium of our human languages. This must surely be one of the reasons why the New Testament teaches us to weigh carefully everything that appears to be revelation. As human beings we are not infallible, we can make mistakes in what we are hearing and even in the manner of our reporting.

Moreover, we are all of us influenced by the things we have been taught, by our culture and background, and none of us is free from openness to deception. The enemy is always prowling around seeking to distort the word of God and to lead us astray. None of us is so holy and sinless that we can say that there is no chink in the whole armour of God around us that allows any access to the enemy. We are flesh and blood and we are no match for the principalities and powers. We do, nevertheless, stand in the victory won for us through the blood of the Lord Jesus, but none of us can claim to be absolutely pure in receiving and handling the contemporary word of God.

God himself has given to us the yardstick of truth in scripture by which to measure the truth of what we are hearing today. It is essential that we learn to use it rightly in our handling of revelation so that the Church is guarded against deception.

The significance of Medjugorje, the other reported appearances of Mary and all the multitude of prophetic messages that are now being received in the Church, lies in the evidence this provides of the great desire of Christians, from every tradition of the Church, to hear God speak to his people today.

There is indeed a new prophetic movement and we need to be aware of all that God is doing among his people in different parts of the world and from different traditions. We need, above all, to understand what is happening today in the context of God fulfilling his promises given to us in the Bible, where we are exhorted both to watch and pray and to be alert to the wiles of the enemy.

Chapter Three

The God Who Teaches Discernment

The Need for Discerning God's Truth

There are millions of Christians today throughout the world who believe they are hearing from God. Prophecy is rapidly becoming the major spiritual characteristic of the age. But it is not the powerful church leaders who are claiming to hear directly from God, but ordinary believers with no leadership responsibilities. This clearly is something to be expected if we are right in our assessment that we are moving into the last days of the present age and therefore seeing a completion of the prophecy of Joel that began to be fulfilled on the day of Pentecost, that God would pour out his Spirit upon all men and women, and they would prophesy. Prophecy, thus envisaged, is a spiritual movement among the people rather than a leadership-led movement. But this openness to divine revelation also opens us to the possibility of deception and we need to learn how to discern between the two. We know from the teaching of Jesus that deception is also a characteristic of the end of the age.

Revelation without discernment leaves the Church highly vulnerable. There is nothing the enemy enjoys more than the spectre of gullible Christians searching for signs and wonders and believing anything supernatural! Satan rubs his hands in glee because he excels in the counterfeit.

The strong emphasis today upon the experiential which has come through the charismatic movement lays the Church open to the intrusion of powerful forces of deception. Our only sure safeguard is to follow closely the teaching of scripture. It is important to notice that discernment is not one of the gifts of the Spirit that is only given to a few. It is available to the whole body of believers – to all who have received the Holy Spirit. This is the teaching of the New Testament.

Paul says that one of the gifts of the Spirit is the "ability to distinguish between spirits" (1 Corinthians 12:10). But this is not the same as discernment. Distinguishing between spirits is a manifestation of the Spirit given to certain individuals, but discernment of spiritual truth is available to all Spirit-filled believers. This is Paul's teaching in 1 Corinthians 2:6–16. He says that "the man without the Spirit does not accept the things that come from the Spirit of God . . . he cannot understand them, because they are spiritually discerned." It is the right of all believers who have been given the Spirit of Truth to be able to discern spiritual truth and thereby to be able to distinguish between truth and error.

The problem of deception is a major one for the Church today due to the lack of biblical teaching on the spiritual gifts and the strong emphasis on everything experiential. It is a problem that has to be faced. Wherever there is prophecy, there is the possibility of deception. This deception is not necessarily deliberate; we can be *sincerely* deceived. The problem is not new – it is as old as prophecy itself.

Even before the time of the great writing prophets of Israel, beginning with Amos in the Eighth Century, false prophecy was a problem. Micaiah had to face the combined witness of four hundred prophets who unanimously advised Jehoshaphat and Ahab that they would be successful in battle against Syria. Micaiah alone had seen "all Israel scattered on the hills like sheep without a shepherd" (1 Kings 22:17). There was no way the two kings could have known which prophecy was right except by putting their confidence in the person of the prophet. Ahab had never found Micaiah prophesying anything good of him so he was prejudiced against him from the start and his word prevailed over Jehoshaphat's caution. There is no record of Micaiah having made any true or false predictions prior to this, so Ahab was probably referring to the prophet having rebuked him in the name of the Lord for his evil ways. The task of the prophet was not simply future prediction but to declare the word of the Lord. Ahab was probably still smarting under the sting of the prophet's rebukes. Now he summarily dismissed Micaiah's warning and he succeeded in persuading Jehoshaphat to follow the advice of the four hundred false prophets. The outcome was a disastrous defeat for both Israel and Judah.

The two kings could only see one way of testing these opposing prophecies which was to see which one was fulfilled. But if they had been men of God such as David or Hezekiah, or even as Jehoshaphat himself was earlier in his life, the Spirit of God within them would have borne witness to the truth and they would have been able to discern which was the true prophecy. This is the function of the Holy Spirit within his servants.

In our own day we have two major ways of testing prophecy. We have the advantage of scripture which was not available to Jehoshaphat and Ahab, and we also have the witness of the Holy Spirit within us which is the gift of the Risen Jesus to his Church.

Even in New Testament times, false prophecy was a problem to the church and for this reason Paul dealt at some length with the subject in his teaching to the Christians in Corinth. The same problem continues to exist for us today and we need to be able to distinguish the false from the genuine. We cannot overemphasise the necessity for following New Testament teaching and practice in regard to the weighing of prophecy in order to guard the Church against deception. (For more detailed teaching on this subject see Clifford Hill, *Prophecy Past and Present*, Highland 1989 pp. 300–4.)

The core of the problem lies in the fact that God wants us to hear from him and he does not want us to be deceived, but his truth is spiritually discerned and we live in a world dominated by secular material values that distort our thinking, distract our attention and blur our spiritual vision. The more we listen to the world, the more difficult it becomes to listen to God. But if we retired from the world to live the life of a recluse, God could not speak to us about the contemporary world situation which would be outside our experience. In any case there would be no point in him speaking to us about something we would be powerless to influence. This would certainly be a case of the word of God returning to him void without having accomplished his purpose. Hence every prophet is caught up in the same dilemma of working within two world systems – that of living within the secular world where God has placed his servants and attempting to shut it out while listening to God; then attempting to identify with the secular world and to interpret the word of God to the understanding of secular man. That is the essence of the problem for all those who long to be part of God's prophetic people.

For the past twenty years there has been an increasing number of prophecies circulating around the world concerning the last days. Many of these have predicted dates for the Rapture, the Second Coming of Christ and other apocalyptic events such as World War III and the Battle of Armageddon. Most of these prophecies have been based upon interpretations of Daniel and Revelation applied uncritically to the contemporary world scene. This type of "prophecy" has appeared in numerous books selling millions of copies dealing with lurid predictions of endtime events, such as cashless societies controlled by "Big Brother" dictators. They forecast the coming, and even the identity, of the antichrist who will take control of the nations, persecute believers and usher in a series of horrendous events leading up to the "judgement of the nations". Many of these prophecies include predictions of the "rapture of the church" at different points in the sequence of events and these have been influential on the thinking of many powerful western leaders.

In an age of fear generated by the rapid pace of social, economic and political change, when many nations possess immense arsenals filled with the most terrifying weapons of destruction, it is a chilling thought that western political, military and international strategy could be influenced by false biblical interpretation. This could even result in leaders thinking that they may be serving God by hastening the Second Coming of Christ through precipitating military action.

With only a few years to go to the end of the Second Millennium, we may expect to see predictions of the end of the world or other apocalyptic events multiply. There were many similar prophecies at the close of the first millennium AD. Today the way has been prepared for an outburst of hysterical prophecies of the end of the world by a multitude of popular books on amateur eschatology that have appeared throughout the past twenty years. The mould was cast in 1970 by the publication of Hal Lindsey's *The Late Great Planet Earth* which is reputed to have sold more than 30 million copies. Typical of this kind of prediction is the statement by Mary Stewart Relfe referring to the 1980s – "This world is now standing on the threshold of the most critical decade in the history of mankind. I had for years charted the end of this world order as closely corresponding to the close of this century. Today, I am not at all certain that one person reading these lines will see 1990 before they see His Eternal Majesty, King Wonderful, Jesus Christ, Son of the Living God, revealed from heaven in flaming fire taking vengeance on them that know not God and obey not the Gospel" (*The 666 System is Here*, 1981 p 61). The book is commended on the back cover by "Colin Deal, author of best-seller, *Christ Returns by 1988*". Comment is hardly necessary!

It is easy enough to pour scorn on these false predictions once the date for their fulfilment has been passed. But millions of people have believed them to be true and have based their lives upon them. This is a clear indication of the woeful lack of sound teaching on prophecy in the churches.

False prophecy can deceive sincere believers and be the cause of personal tragedy such as in the case of the nine hundred men, women and children who committed mass suicide in the jungles of Guyana upon the instructions of the Reverend Jim Jones. It is worth noting that he began his ministry as an ordinary Baptist preacher before becoming a cult leader. We are all of us liable to go off the track into error. But we are part of the body of Christ and we need each other as a check on our biblical interpretation and doctrine. When we start acting in isolation we are in grave danger of being deceived.

False prophecy can have the far-reaching effect of undermining the faith of many other believers and bringing the whole subject of prophecy into disrepute. This can result in the out-of-hand rejection of all revelation and the failure to recognise the significance of the times and what the Spirit is saying to the churches today. This can serve to hinder the work of the Holy Spirit and to frustrate God's plans for a prophetic people in our day.

By contrast with the "doom and gloom" prophecies of impending apocalyptic holocausts enveloping the world, there are also many prophecies circulating among the western nations today of imminent revival. These prophecies are immensely popular with growing numbers of believers because of their message of peace and joy and the hope of good things instead of the world of violence that is constantly thrust upon us through the news media. These prophecies speak of God's intervention through a new outpouring of the Holy Spirit in signs and wonders that will give believers incredible supernatural powers. The prophecies, like those predicting the judgement of the nations, are often specific, even naming dates and places where revival will break out and spread across whole nations and continents. A number of these dates came and went in the 1980s and many more are predicted for the 1990s.

These "revival prophecies" create a problem similar to that of the "judgement prophecies" in that they not only build up false expectations but can actually distract believers from understanding the true purposes of God for his people by building up false hopes. They result in people preparing for the wrong thing and thus being unprepared for events that actually do happen. This can also cause people to lose confidence in prophecy.

If God is wanting to prepare his people for battle, when they are excitedly expecting revival, the Church will not be armed with the right weapons and ready to face the situation. If God is calling his people to repentance, when they are only hearing messages calling them to celebrations of praise and rejoicing in God's blessing upon the righteous, they are not going to be a cleansed and purified people whom God can use. He is calling for a people who are separated from the contaminating influences of the world at a critical period in history when God is beginning to move in power against the principalities driving the nations towards destruction.

The point we are emphasising is that when the prophets get the message wrong, and the people are misled on a massive scale, the results can be horrendous; a whole generation can miss the timing of the Lord as for example happened in Judah in the time of Jesus. Jesus himself wept over Jerusalem when he saw the consequences of their rejection of him because they did not recognise the time of God's visitation (Luke 19:41–44).

Throughout his ministry Jeremiah wrestled with the problems generated by false prophets who filled the people with false hopes of peace when God was warning them of the battles that would soon encompass the land and lead to the destruction even of Jerusalem itself. Jeremiah's message was that this did not have to happen. It was only inevitable if the people refused to heed the warnings God was sending to them concerning the consequence of their own unrighteousness. So long as they continued to listen to the false prophets giving them a message of peace and telling them there was nothing wrong with the nation, they would see no necessity for repentance and this would make the destruction of Jerusalem certain. This was the agony Jeremiah faced because he alone foresaw clearly what would happen and his was the lone voice against a multitude of popular preachers telling the people the very things they wanted to hear.

Through Jeremiah, God said, "A horrible and shocking thing has happened in the land: the prophets prophesy lies, the priests rule by their own authority, and my people love it this way. But what will you do in the end? . . . From the least to the greatest, all are greedy for gain; prophets and priests alike, all practise deceit. They dress the wound of my people as though it were not serious. 'Peace, peace',

55

they say, when there is no peace" (Jeremiah 5:30–31, 6:13–14). The false prophets did not perceive the danger facing the nation. They actually believed that Jerusalem was inviolable because it was the Holy City, but Jeremiah knew that God would not protect an unrighteous people.

The situation today throughout the western nations is very similar to the time of Jeremiah, with many popular prophecies in circulation promising revival and times of great spiritual blessing that are exciting the people. These are just the kind of things people want to hear – "my people love it this way" – this can still be said of us today. But the spiritual state of the Church is one of great immaturity, unbelief and apostasy. The false prophets ignore this and it is still true today that "they dress the wound of my people as though it were not serious". It is no good saying "Peace, peace" if the Lord is saying "There is no peace". It is wrong to build up the hopes of people for easy revival without speaking of the cost. It is no good promising great blessings if the Lord is calling for repentance and turning to him in humility, penitence and trust.

The Signs Today

One of the major reasons why false prophecy abounds today is the lack of understanding of prophecy. The popular idea of the prophet is of one who foretells the future whereas the biblical concept of the prophet is of one who is the mouthpiece of God. The prophet is not a fortune-teller but one who declares the word of God with divine power and authority. Prophecy is not simply predicting future events but perceiving the spiritual significance of what is happening today and what God is conveying to his people in the contemporary situation.

It is the prediction of the future that catches the popular

imagination, yet it is this supernatural element that is most likely to distort the understanding of prophecy and to detract from the message that is the whole purpose of divine revelation. The biblical prophets devoted very little of their ministry to predicting the future. Their major concern was to understand contemporary events, especially those that they discerned as "the deeds of the Lord", and to declare to the people what God was saying to them in the immediate situation.

In testing prophecy it is always useful to ask the question, Why would God reveal this? For example, if someone predicts a drought, you have to ask why God would give this foreknowledge. There has to be some spiritual significance and it is this message, or interpretation of the event, that the prophet is called upon to declare. The significance lies not in the accurate prediction but in the interpretation. Today, many people have reversed this and get very excited about "accurate predictions" because they are more interested in "signs and wonders" than in the true purpose of prophecy.

In biblical times if God did give foreknowledge of future events it was always for a purpose, to enable adequate preparations to be made, as, for example, when Joseph prepared for the seven years of famine (Genesis 41:28–32), or when Jehoshaphat was given the exact direction of the enemy assault through the prophet Jahaziel so that he was able to go out to meet the opposing army in the knowledge that God was completely in control (2 Chronicles 20:14–17). God does not give us knowledge of the future simply to enable us to know more than our secular neighbours but only where it is essential for the fulfilling of his purposes.

Sometimes God gives revelation in order to enable us to understand a past event. This is the most common form of revelation that prophets receive. The Old Testament prophets regularly got before the Lord to seek understanding of current events, and this is what we should be doing today with those things that are occupying the attention of the nation to ask God if they are "a sign". If they are a sign we need to know the interpretation, so that the spiritual significance can be conveyed to the people.

This is how signs are often used in scripture. In biblical language a "sign" is not always a "miracle" as it is in the Fourth Gospel, but it can be an everyday event with a spiritual meaning. For example, Jesus referred to the accident that everyone in Jerusalem was talking about – the collapse of a tower in the Siloam area of the city which killed eighteen people. Jesus was careful to avoid saying that it was God who was directly responsible for the disaster. It was a human accident, although clearly God had allowed it, and Jesus picked up the spiritual significance of the human negligence (greed, exploitation or some other sin) that lay behind the accident and used it as an illustration of the precarious situation of the nation in his day. Sudden destruction would undoubtedly befall the city of Jerusalem unless there was repentance and a turning to God. It would be just as sudden and unexpected as the collapse of the Tower of Siloam (Luke 13:4–5). In Luke's Gospel, Jesus' reference to the tragedy of Siloam follows immediately after his rebuke to the people for not knowing how to interpret the signs of the times. He uses the accident as a powerful illustration of his teaching.

The ministry team, of which we are a part, regularly gets before the Lord to seek understanding of any events that are currently in the news. The whole ministry of *Prophecy Today* is founded upon this understanding of prophecy. The magazine firmly resists the temptation to get into predicting dates and times, especially in regard to the fulfilment of biblical prophecy, which is something Jesus warned his disciples to avoid. Our generation is saturated with news media comment and opinions on current events, but rarely seeks any spiritual interpretation. Secular men do not recognise the need to see things from God's perspective.

Occasionally, however, even the media are baffled for any explanation other than "an act of God", such as when York Minster was struck by lightning within hours of the consecration in that building of David Jenkins as Bishop of Durham. There was great speculation in the press that God had sent a sign of his displeasure to the Church because of the unorthodox theological views expressed by the new bishop who was reported as doubting (or denying) some of the fundamentals of the Christian faith. Those who denied most vehemently that God had deliberately set fire to the Minster, were the two top leaders of the Church of England, the Archbishops of Canterbury and York, who each declared that God does not act in this way. It was a rare example of the secular media being more open to belief in divine action than church leaders – although the incident was probably more revealing for lack of faith within the Church than for a new found faith in the media!

There have been many other signs that have had a clear spiritual interpretation for British people in recent years, especially in regard to greed and corruption in economic affairs. The sinking of the cross-channel ferry at Zeebrugge, with the loss of nearly two hundred lives, was an accident that should never have happened. It occurred because the ferry sailed with its bow doors open in order to save time on the turn around, thus maximising profits to the owners regardless of safety considerations. Where increasing profits become more important than human life, there is a clear need for an unequivocal declaration of the word of God who hates greed and exploitation. The hurricane that struck

South-East England (the most prosperous area of Britain) caused the closure of the London Stock Exchange which triggered off the worldwide crash of the Stock Market in October 1987 (as reported in *Prophecy Today*, Vol 4, No 1, p 6) was another clear sign of God's anger at the injustice and avarice upon which the whole western economy is founded.

It is not easy to explain away a hurricane in southern Britain. The last one to hit that part of the UK was in 1703 – the year John Wesley was born. Forty years later the great Wesleyan revival began that swept across Britain and transformed the nation's life. Out of the turmoil of industrial anarchy, social violence and moral decay, the spiritual revival generated by the Wesleys changed the course of history and saved Britain from the horrors of civil war and the kind of bloody revolution that occurred in France. Many people today are longing to see God move in power upon the nation in a similar way and are praying for this to happen.

But God has to prepare the way for his own sovereign acts of salvation. He does this by preparing his people and arming them for the struggle against the entrenched forces of the enemy that have possessed the land. In Britain today there are powerful forces of spiritual evil that have taken a stronghold in the life of the nation. God is raising an army of alert "watchmen" who are able to discern these things. And he often uses some outstanding occurrence to alert us to the significance of enemy activity as has often happened in our experience.

In January 1989 I took part in a radio programme with the Bishop of Durham and others. It was called *Acts of God* and was a discussion of whether or not God acts today in the same way as he is reported to have done in biblical times; and whether or not it is true that many of the events happening today have a spiritual interpretation as the "deeds of the Lord" a spiritual interpretation as the "deeds of the Lord" through which God conveys a message to us. The programme which was broadcast on 8th January 1989 ended with the lightning strike that set fire to York Minster. The noise of thunder was heard as the programme faded out. This was immediately followed by an announcer's voice saying that an aircraft had crashed on the M1 motorway in Leicestershire and warning motorists to avoid the area. The announcement was so dramatic in its timing that it appeared to many listeners to be part of the programme.

The peculiar circumstances surrounding this crash as well as the timing of the announcement caused me to seek the Lord earnestly in the following days for understanding.

The media were full of reports of fire in one of the engines of this brand new aeroplane but that the pilot had shut down the wrong engine. As I prayed about this I continually heard the word "confusion". This was later confirmed during the public enquiry where recorded conversations between the pilot and co-pilot were reported. There was indecision on the flight deck as to which engine had been trouble and in the end the wrong decision was made. As I continued to seek the Lord for understanding of this I was shown in a vision a picture of the runway and the countryside beyond. I could see fields, then woodland and then a clearing in the woods. My attention was drawn to the clearing that I estimated to be about a mile beyond the runway and immediately in line with it. I saw a bizarre scene of witches dancing in a circle and I heard incantations that reminded me of the witches' scene from Macbeth. I could see the "confusion" being radiated towards the stricken incoming plane and

I felt I was being shown the cause of the confusion on the flight deck.

Some time later I asked one of our prayer partners, who lives near to the East Midlands Airport, if she knew what lay just beyond the western end of the runway. I myself have never been to that area but I described to her in detail what I had seen – a wooded area with a clearing in which there was a witches' coven and then a further wooded area beyond. At that stage I had not even consulted a map to confirm the geographical features that I had seen. She volunteered to obtain an ordnance map of the area and to go and investigate with three others who regularly prayed with her. There were no roads in the area so they had to walk across fields to reach the point a mile to the west of the runway. They found the two areas of woodland just as I had described with a clearing, in the middle of which were two dead trees, and a large oak tree the top of which had also been struck by lightning. On the ground around its trunk there had been placed a circle of large stones surrounded by a circle of well-trodden earth. Hanging from one of the lower branches was a large dead bird with its wings outstretched suspended by string, and a skeleton of another bird also tied to a branch by string.

I asked the Lord why he had revealed this to me especially as the crash had already occurred and there was nothing I could do to prevent the disaster. The answer I was given was that the Lord was alerting me to the increasing danger of occultism and the devastating effects that witchcraft is beginning to have in Britain. Not since the Middle Ages has there been such an amount of occultic activity in Europe.

Recent statistics show that there are more witches than church ministers registered in West Germany, and more witches than priests in France. Witches are not registered in Britain but there is evidence from newspaper reports from every part of the country that the position in Britain is very similar. Local newspapers regularly carry reports of the revival of Druid practices in rural areas and of the activities of witches' covens. More worryingly, there often appear in the national press lurid reports of satanist rites linked with child sexual abuse and even child sacrifice.

The Lord is wanting to alert his people to the significance of this onslaught from the principalities and powers of darkness. The situation is far more serious than most Christians realise. It is a result of the repealing of the Witchcraft Act some thirty years ago, and the liberalising of laws governing censorship of publications and the arts, that has allowed a flood of pornography and violence to become common-place in Britain and throughout Europe. This, together with the general decline in morality, and the breakdown of family and marriage that has accompanied a widespread loss of faith and decline in church attendance, has produced this turning of the nation back to its old pagan roots. Britain is a nation that has acknowledged the sovereignty of God and the authority of the Bible in all its institutions for many centuries. Thus, this turning away from God is an act of apostasy that is abhorrent to him and he is calling upon those who still acknowledge his Lordship to recognise the danger facing the nation and to be ready to combat it.

Discerning God's Heart

God is showing us that we are in a situation of war, but as Paul points out "We do not wage war as the world does. The weapons we fight with are not the weapons of the world" but God has given us the Holy Spirit which puts spiritual weapons into our hands which "have divine power to demolish strongholds" (2 Corinthians 10:3–4). God is mobilising an army of his people for battle. This is the Gideon's Army about which so many believers have been receiving prophetic words in recent years. It is an army in which the infantry are intercessors.

God is mobilising a great company of strong intercessors throughout the world and it is for this reason that we are seeing such an emphasis upon prayer among Christians in every nation. Many churches report that the prayer meeting, which used to be the most poorly attended, is now the focal point of the life of the fellowship. In those churches where the leadership have a real vision for what God is doing today, it is actually an exciting experience to be present at the prayer meeting. When the Holy Spirit is sought for the "prayer agenda" as well as for the direction of the whole meeting, there is a corporate realisation of the presence of the Lord Jesus among his people and the "church militant" becomes not just a phrase in a creed but a living experience.

This new emphasis upon prayer has been growing throughout the past two or three decades not only in Britain but around the world. In many nations there are organisations linking together those who pray regularly for the churches and for those involved in government and social and economic affairs in the life of their nation. There are many of these intercessory networks whose members meet in small groups of three or four, or slightly larger groups of ten or twelve, on a daily or weekly basis for prayer. These networks usually provide them with information on current affairs and give guidance for specific prayer themes. Another characteristic of these small prayer cells is their interdenominational character; the urge to pray is being experienced by Christians from many different traditions of the Church. The prayer networks often call their members together for days of prayer and fasting in response to specific moral or social issues which is a further sign of the recognition today of the power of prayer.

Even persecution cannot stop Christians praying – this was acknowledged by Albania in May 1990 when the Albanian Government said that it was no longer illegal to believe in God. Forty-five years of Communist rule had been unable to to stop people believing in God.

In many of the nations that have recently been experiencing a new move of God in evangelism, such as has occurred throughout South East Asia, the emphasis upon the power of prayer is foremost. This is particularly to be seen in countries like China where the authorities have been persecuting the believers for many years.

South Korea, that has survived a devastating war and has lived under threat from the North for forty years, has during this period experienced rapid growth of the faith in a society which had very few Christians. South Korea is known today for its mega-churches but what is often not recognised is that the power behind these very large congregations is the power of prayer and the multitude of small prayer groups. Individuals also make prayer a regular part of their personal devotional life using what are known as "prayer mountains" – places of solitude devoted to private intercession.

Prayer comes more naturally to those from a non-western background especially to those who have come out of the contemplative religions such as Buddhism. There is, however, no excuse for this for westerners with their Judaeo/Christian background, for prayer lay at the heart of the ministry exercised by the prophets in ancient Israel. The prophets were the intercessors for the nation. They carried the burden of the contemporary situation into the presence of the Lord and not only sought for his word but also pleaded on behalf of the people.

There are many examples in scripture of this, such as when Amos pleaded with God on behalf of Israel when he heard God saying that he would bring destruction upon the land. In a vision he saw a swarm of locusts devastating the land. "When they had stripped the land clean, I cried out, 'Sovereign Lord, forgive! How can Jacob survive? He is so small!' So the Lord relented. 'This will not happen', the Lord said" (Amos 7:2–3). Amos was shown three pictures of judgement coming upon the nation. The second was a picture of fire sweeping across the land. Again he interceded on behalf of the people and God stayed his hand. The third picture, which presumably was seen some time later, was of the Lord standing with a plumb line in his hand and when the prophet saw this he knew that there was no point in further pleading with God. The previous warnings had been ignored, the whole life of the nation was so corrupt that the plumb line of the Lord revealed the depth of corruption into which the whole nation had sunk. God could no longer spare them without denying the righteousness of his own nature, so Amos was silent. The prophetic silence is more deafening than the prophet's denunciation.

The account of Amos's three visions is a good example of the way revelation, discernment and intercession go together. When the prophet gets into the presence of the Lord he is able to discern the true state of the nation because he is seeing things through the eyes of God and not through human eyes. This depth of spiritual insight is a result of revelation; discernment enables the prophet to know what is on the heart of the Lord and thus to pray in accordance with the will of God. If he discerns that God is grieving over the state of the nation and longing to forgive, then the call to repentance will be declared with great passion while at the same time the prophet's intercession will be a fervent plea for the Lord to stay his hand in compassion and to give more time for the nation to come to repentance.

Revelation, discernment and intercession are still linked today and are inseparable parts of the prophetic ministry into which God is calling all his people. God is longing for his people to be a prophetic people, to whom he can speak through revelation, who will exercise discernment through the Holy Spirit, and who will faithfully intercede before him on behalf of the Church and nation. We have already noted that revelation and discernment are given for a purpose and are not given to us merely so that we can play with the spiritual gifts or exercise spiritual one-upmanship over other Christians! When God gives us special revelation, it is in order that we may carry out his purposes. The obligation is then laid upon us to discover what he wants us to do and how he wants us to do it.

This was brought home to us forcefully during one of our Team Ministry engagements in the West Midlands of England. The meetings were being held in Wolver-hampton and when the Team arrived on the Thursday they found the whole town in ferment over an incident that had just occurred in which a young man had been caught allegedly using a stolen credit card in a department store. The police had been called and during a forcible arrest the young man died. He was from the local West Indian community so that the incident had immediate implications threatening the racial harmony of the area.

The following day it was announced that there would be a demonstration on the Saturday with a march through the town led by prominent members of the local black community including the black pastors of local churches. They were protesting at what they saw as a grave act of injustice by the police in using unnecessary force that ended the young man's life. It also became known that many political activists from other inner-city areas such as Bristol, Birmingham and London were intending coming to take part in the demonstration. The reports indicated that these groups were coming intent on violence and there were threats to "burn the town down".

We ourselves arrived in the town to join the Team on the Friday in time for an evening public meeting in the Town Hall. We met with local Christian leaders before this meeting to decide whether or not to carry on with the weekend programme, which included a number of seminars in churches that were on the route of the proposed march. We decided to turn the Friday evening meeting into a prayer meeting and the Team, together with hundreds of local believers, urgently sought the Lord to know what we should be doing in this confusing situation. Sympathies were divided, we wanted to stand with our black brothers and sisters, to grieve with them in their sadness (the young man who had died came from one of the black Pentecostal families), while at the same time we did not want to be identified with social anarchy that would have brought us into confrontation with the forces of law and order. We wished to express our deep concern for justice and our abhorrence of the loss of this young man's life, while at the same time we had no wish to become involved in a riot.

We cried out to the Lord for wisdom in this difficult situation to which we could see no clear answer. We recognised that it was the outsiders coming into the town who were the real threat to law and order that could turn a peaceful demonstration into a riotous assembly because their agenda was different. We prayed the prayer of Jehoshaphat, "Lord, we do not know what to do, but our eyes are upon you" (2 Chronicles 20:12). The Lord answered by revealing to us that the threatened riot would not take place, that he would act sovereignly in such a way that would allow the peaceful demonstration to take place but prevent any outbreak of social violence. God did not show us how he was going to do this, but he spoke so clearly that we received the word in faith. Sometimes God does not show us the detail of what he intends to do because he wants us to act in faith.

All the believers went home that Friday night with joy and confidence in the Lord who had promised that he would act the next day. We were also told that the programme of meetings had to continue but the teaching programme at the Baptist Church, opposite the police station where the arresting officers were based, had to be abandoned and replaced by a meeting for intercession and witness. This was not to take place behind closed doors but out in the street in full view of the public. It so happened that I was scheduled to teach the seminars at this church and it was clearly right for me to lead the prayer meeting.

In the early hours of Saturday morning the Lord began to fulfil his promise; a snow storm descended upon Wolverhampton! The town awoke to find itself wrapped in a blanket of several inches of snow and blizzard conditions which continued right through the morning. It had been a mild winter and this was already early springtime and the last thing anyone expected was to see snow. But the most remarkable thing was that the snow only fell upon Wolverhampton and an area of about ten miles around the town. Even in Birmingham, less than twenty miles away, there was no snow. The town of Wolverhampton was cut off. The roads leading off the motorway were impassable and the coachloads of "troublemakers" from the inner-city areas of other conurbations were unable to get through. We did not know this until later, but we believed the word God had given us that the demonstration would pass off peacefully and that there would be a sign from him that would bring honour to his name.

Outside the Baptist Church, a company of believers began singing praises to the Lord several hours before the march was due to pass that point. Inside the church, others were keeping up a constant stream of intercession. Police had been drafted in from all over the West Midlands to line the streets along the entire route and a wall of grim-faced mounted police guarded the police station opposite the church. Television cameras were there to record the expected violence and as the time of the demonstration approached, the tension heightened.

With an hour to go I left the group of prayer and praise warriors who were making their presence known throughout the street with passers-by joining the singing and members of the group seizing many opportunities for personal evangelism. I went up and down the street along the line of mounted police and those on foot, speaking to each man individually, most of whom looked tense and nervous. I assured each man that God had sent the snow as a sign of his sovereignty and in fulfilment of the promise he had given us in the Town Hall the previous night that he would ensure that the demonstration would pass peacefully. The riot everyone was expecting (and the media were eagerly awaiting!) would not take place. There would be no violence that day and no one would be hurt. We learned later that this message was broadcast on the police transmitter right across the West Midlands region an hour before the march began.

Some three thousand people took part in the demonstration instead of the expected thirty thousand who would have been there if it had not been for the snow storm. The demonstration was a purely local expression of deep concern about injustice. Black and white people took part, many of them from local churches and the march was led by black Pentecostal pastors. There was no violence throughout the entire length of the march, even at the most tense point along the route outside the police station; there was a lot of shouting but the most violent acts were the throwing of a few snowballs.

The Saturday night meeting in the Town Hall which was to have been on the theme *The Word of God for Our Times* became a great celebration event. God had already demonstrated that he does have a word for our times. His word is powerful and he is able to meet every situation. It was reported to the meeting by a local police inspector, who was a believer, that the police throughout the region were talking about the amazing events of that day and he had already heard of one man who had given his life to the Lord as a result of what had happened.

When God acts, he acts in power to achieve his purposes. The outcome of that day was not simply the preservation of law and order in the town, but the promotion of greater harmony in race relations and unity among believers from the black and white churches. This clearly was something that was on the Father's heart and he used this incident to achieve his purposes. But the good purposes of God can be frustrated if his people are not listening to him, discerning what is on his heart, and prepared to act in faith. Revelation, discernment and intercession all played a part in bringing about what was widely reported, even in the secular media, as "The Miracle of Wolverhampton".

Chapter Four

The God Who Speaks Personally

God is undoubtedly speaking to his people today. But this is nothing new. There never was a time when God was not speaking to his people, to those who were open to hear from him. Jeremiah says "From the time your forefathers left Egypt until now, day after day, again and again, I sent you my servants the prophets" (7:25). The opening statement of Hebrews declares a similar message that God had spoken in the past "to our forefathers through the prophets at many times and in various ways, but in these last days he has spoken to us by his Son" (Hebrews 1:1–2).

Personal Messages from God

God has always spoken through individuals but in this chapter we are not considering God's use of individuals through whom he revealed his nature and purposes as he did through the great prophets of Israel. Neither are we thinking about his use of individuals through whom he conveyed a prophetic message to the nation or to the Church. We are looking at God speaking personally into the lives of individuals, either directly to that person or through another individual. This is our understanding of personal prophecy.

Much of the emphasis in the new prophetic movement today is on personal prophecy. This also was true of the early days of the Pentecostal movement at the beginning of this century. Some of the Pentecostal churches such as the Apostolic Church of God and the Church of God of Prophecy have retained this emphasis on prophecy. But these churches do not only expect revelation for individual lives; their major emphasis is upon God's direction of the Church and its ministry.

The expansion of the charismatic movement has placed a fresh emphasis upon individual spiritual gifts which has resulted in millions of Spirit-filled believers looking to the Lord to speak into their lives in a personal way. They are open to receiving a message through their times of personal Bible study, devotion and intercession, and to God speaking to them through the message of a preacher or through times of worship, listening to teaching tapes, or in small group prayer meetings as well as privately through dreams, visions and everyday events. They are also open to receiving messages from others and for others.

Many Spirit-filled believers who are exercising prophetic gifts have experienced rejection within the Church as well as from secular authorities to whom they have tried to communicate the words they have been receiving. Thus it may be that part of the reason for the current emphasis upon personal prophecy is that it has been born out of frustration. Personal prophecy is more acceptable within the limited sphere of the small group arena than in the wider field where its implications have greater consequences.

The value of personal prophecy is that God is able to use it, according to the level of faith within the individual, to guide that person's life. God's promise to his servants who trust him is "whether you turn to the right or to the left, your ears will hear a voice behind you, saying, 'This is the way; walk in it'" (Isaiah 30:21). It should be the earnest desire of every believer to learn to listen to the voice of God speaking to us through his Spirit. There are really two parts to this: the one is to recognise when God is speaking to us and the ways in which he communicates with us, and the second part is to discern or interpret what the Spirit is saying.

There is nothing new in the fact of God communicating with his people: the new thing is the vast numbers of believers who, through the fulfilling of what Joel saw would take place in the last days (the outpouring of the Spirit upon all people) are actually hearing from God today. Millions of ordinary people can testify to the life changing experience that the coming of the Holy Spirit into their lives has made. But this has always been true. When God breaks into a person's life he makes an amazing transformation. Jesus speaks of it as being "born again" and Paul refers to it as becoming "a new creation". The effect is to walk by faith and no longer to walk in the ways of the world.

All the great heroes of the faith in the Old Testament were distinguished by their faith in God. This is the point made in Hebrews 11 which even includes the "prostitute Rahab" along with "Gideon, Barak, Samson, Jephthah, David, Samuel and the prophets" among those "whose weakness was turned to strength" by the Spirit of God coming upon them (vv 31–34). They were ordinary people until the Spirit made them extraordinary and enabled them to do extraordinary deeds.

From my earliest childhood I was raised on the stories of these great men and women of God. I was not raised on Noddy or Toytown tales but on Bible stories of the heroes of the faith and it was everyday experience to me that God, who had spoken in former times through the prophets, was still speaking to us today through his Son. My mother was a godly woman whose whole life was devoted to the Lord. God had spoken to her while I was still in the womb telling her that she would give birth to a male child who would serve him. She received this and other promises as a solemn commission from the Lord to prepare me for the day when God would speak to me. At the moment of my birth she took me in her arms and dedicated me to the Lord.

When I was twelve God spoke to me personally for the first time and told me that he had called me to be his servant and that I was to be a preacher of the Word and through me he would speak to the people. It was after I recounted this experience to my parents that I was told what the Lord had said to my mother before I was born. Two years later, as a fourteen-year-old school boy, I began preaching in village churches accompanied in the early days by an elderly lay preacher who had perceived the Spirit of God upon me and who had taken me under his wing. I have been preaching the Gospel regularly ever since that day.

Right up to the time I entered Theological College I accepted it as a normal everyday experience of believers that God would be speaking to us personally. It was an intense spiritual shock to find others in college with me who did not believe that God speaks today and also many who were entering the Church as a profession having not received any personal experience of a call of God upon their lives. In fact some of my professors did not even believe that God had ever spoken! My theological education was a painful experience and after I was ordained it took me some years to recover my faith in a living personal God who communicates clearly with his people. At no stage did I doubt my call to ministry and I was a faithful pastor and a passionate preacher of the Gospel. I was highly involved in prophetic action both in the church and in the community which often gained national publicity. But it was not until I received a fresh outpouring of the Holy Spirit upon my life through an experience of brokenness that I regained a vital sense of the presence of the Living God speaking to me in a personal way.

Covenanting for a Purpose

The relationship with a God who speaks personally, is basic to biblical Christianity. The history of God's dealings with the Children of Israel was founded upon a personal relationship that was established in the time of Abraham. The covenant was "I will be your God and you will be my people". This actually applied to the whole nation of Israel but it became personalised through the Lord Jesus Christ which was a fulfilment of what Jeremiah foresaw as the "New Covenant" that God would establish with his people whereby each one would know God for themselves (Jeremiah 31:31).

A covenant by definition has a two-way set of promises and obligations which have to be entered into voluntarily by both parties. God is continually offering his new covenant of love to each of his children in every generation. But we have to enter into this personal relationship with God through an act of commitment which puts upon us the obligation of trust and obedience as servants of the Lord Jesus. It is this act of commitment that puts us into a covenant relationship with God whereby he is able to speak to us personally.

It is in fulfilment of his covenant promises that God

speaks to us and therefore he always speaks for a purpose. The major reasons why God will speak to us are:

- to give guidance for the right direction of our lives;
- to correct, rebuke or redirect us at critical points in our lives;
- to tell us about things that may happen in the future to enable us to be forewarned;
- to prepare us for mission and service; and
- to increase our faith and build us up to greater spiritual maturity.

We will look at each of these in more detail with both biblical and present-day examples, noting especially the three important aspects of every kind of prophecy – revelation, interpretation and application.

a) Guidance

Abraham had learned to trust God and to be in communication with him long before the covenant was formalised. God's purpose in speaking to him personally was to give him guidance and prepare him to be the father of a nation whom he would use. God told him "all peoples on earth will be blessed through you" (Genesis 12:3). At that time he gave Abraham a specific direction "leave your country, your people and your father's household and go to the land I will show you" (Genesis 12:1). To obey such a command required enormous trust in God and confidence that he was hearing him rightly, because it meant stepping out alone into the unknown and leaving behind him the protection of his family and tribe.

This same direct guidance is available to us today through the Holy Spirit. God has not changed – he will still speak to those who seek him and who earnestly desire to know him so that he can work out his good plans for our lives. In Jeremiah's words these are "plans to give you hope and a future" (Jeremiah 29:11).

In fact any who claim to belong to the Lord and who make their own plans without seeking his face to know his will for their lives, are regarded by God as "obstinate children" according to Isaiah 30:1. "Woe to the obstinate children, declares the Lord, to those who carry out plans that are not mine ... who go down to Egypt without consulting me." God expects us to consult him in everything – even in the smallest details of our lives.

If we get used to doing this in the small things then we will be able to hear him when we are faced with momentous decisions. We have tried to do this throughout our married life. For each new phase of ministry we have sought God's specific guidance and asked him to guard us against running ahead with our own "good ideas". We have also learned to trust him for his perfect timing in any change we have had to face. It has always been our experience that each time we moved house, it has not only been right for us and for the ministry but has also been right for each of our three children. God is a God of detail and he makes sure that all things work together for the good of those who love him (Romans 8:28). In fact we have learned never to take any initiative until God has given us a specific sign to confirm his word. If ever we have been unsure, we have always asked him to stop us from going ahead with any plans that are not his and we have found that God is faithful both in detail and in timing.

I grew up with this experience of God speaking personally in my family life. I was a child during the war and my family remained in London throughout the heavy bombing as my father was in charge of the telephone communications between London, Washington and the Allied Military Headquarters, and my mother wouldn't leave him, neither would she be parted from her children. As a family, each day we sought the Lord's protection as the destruction intensified around us, and each day we received the Lord's assurance that he was watching over us.

Then one day my mother said that the Lord had spoken to her and shown her that the time had come to move. Within a week we moved to another part of London, where the Lord had said we would be safe, and six days after moving, the house we had just left was destroyed by a bomb in our street. My parents had taken into our family a homeless young man semi-paralysed with multiple sclerosis whom they had found wandering the streets in an old self-propelled wheelchair without money and without food. He was unable to get down into our back garden shelter and he used to sleep on a bed in our front room downstairs. There is no doubt that he would have been killed if my mother had not been given the word to move. We always believed that the Lord told us to move for the sake of this young man and not to protect our home. He preserved us as a family because we had blessed a homeless and helpless young man. He died about two years later but he went to be with the Lord as a believer who had experienced the love of the Lord through the sacrificial love of my parents. As a child I learned the lesson that God's blessings are not given to us for selfish advantage but come as a result of our self-giving in loving service.

This is a lesson we try always to keep firmly in mind when seeking for a word from the Lord for personal guidance. God does not hand out his blessings simply to give us an advantage over our unbelieving neighbours or to shower material riches upon us for our comfort. Of course, he will bless us with the things we need and will do so abundantly, but the key to asking rightly is to ensure that we are in the centre of his will. Once we have that assurance we will only ask for those things that are in accordance with his will and we can make our requests in complete faith knowing that he will grant them.

Far too many people today are looking for guidance before they have established a right relationship with the Lord which can lead to accepting guidance through others and not receiving direct confirmation from the Lord for themselves.

Another of the trends in the charismatic movement is the intrusion of the individualism of western society into the Church. There is a concentration on "me and my needs" and guidance for MY life rather than what God wants me to do or the needs of others. All too often the emphasis in charismatic communities is very self-centred and self-gratifying. It is seeking God for his blessing upon me, my family, my health and my finances. Even our spirituality reflects Western individualism. The current charismatic emphasis upon "holiness" is usually a subjective relationship rather than an objective seeking for God to direct our energies, gifts and resources into creative and self-giving service.

b) Correction and Rebuke

God sometimes speaks to us to give correction where we are going wrong or where we have not been rightly seeking his guidance. Provided we have been faithful in our love of the Lord and our desire to be in a right relationship with him, even if we have acted foolishly or run ahead without seeking his plans for a particular period in our lives, he will find a way of bringing correction to us. God sometimes not only has to redirect our lives, which may be painful, but also has to bring a rebuke.

David is a clear example of a servant of the Lord who was rebuked for his personal behaviour. David really loved the Lord and must have been perfectly well aware of his sin in planning the death of Uriah to cover his adultery with the man's wife, but he was unwilling to face it. It took the courage of the prophet Nathan to make David acknowledge his wrong-doing and come to repentance. The phrase "Thou art the man!" is an accusation that still comes to us centuries later with an awesome ring. David accepted the rebuke in humility and wept before the Lord, confessing his sin and asking for forgiveness and so it was not long before he was restored to a right relationship with God.

God sometimes has to use others to get his message through to us because of our blindness or our unwillingness to face up to things that are wrong in our personal lives. It is always easier to see the offences of others than to recognise sin in ourselves which was the point of Jesus' reference to taking the log out of your own eye in order to be able to see clearly the splinter in someone else's eye. A modern illustration of this startled the world when American tele-evangelist Jim Bakker made accusations against Jimmy Swaggart who led a similar ministry. Later the finger of accusation was pointed against Jim Bakker, and following investigation of his financial affairs and personal morality he was publicly humiliated and imprisoned.

The greater responsibility we have, the more devastating the consequences of our wrong-doing. King David discovered this when he fell for the sin of pride in numbering the fighting men of the nation. Once he repented he was willing to bear the responsibility personally, but he had involved the whole nation in his action and therefore there were national consequences. A plague swept the nation that was only halted on the outskirts of

Jerusalem where David built an altar of intercession.

God's rebukes are always in love and always with the offer of forgiveness even though there may be certain inevitable consequences that cannot be avoided. None of us are isolated individuals and when we do wrong it does affect the lives of others. The greater responsibility we bear, the more lives are affected. When the pastor of a church falls into adultery, as has been happening with increasing frequency in recent years, it affects the whole congregation and many others, and is a set back to evangelism as it brings the name of the Lord into disrepute. One church near our home in London has had three successive ministries break down through the adultery of the pastors – surely a devastating experience for a Bible-believing congregation.

God is using prophecy to speak into these situations where his servants are deaf to his personal word of rebuke. Increasingly he is giving greater boldness to those with prophetic insight to deal with this situation, whereby the values of the world have intruded into the church. John Wimber tells how Paul Cain was used by the Lord to reveal to him accurate information about the adulterous behaviour of some of those in leadership positions at the Vineyard in Anaheim where he is the Senior Pastor. John Wimber confesses that he himself had not been hearing clearly from the Lord for some time due to the pressures and demands of an expanding international ministry. He was aware that there were things that were not right in his church but he trusted those in senior positions of leadership around him and he was not open to hearing anything against them. It is under these circumstances that prophetic revelation plays a vital part in ministry. God is calling for a holy people cleansed from the adulterous practices of the world; from the lying, cheating and greed that surrounds us in this generation. He wants a people who are wholly committed to him in love, in trust and in obedience.

Prophecy can, however, be misused in regard to prophetic revelation of sin in the church. Where God gives to those exercising prophetic gifts knowledge of specific sins in a congregation, these should not be revealed in public without first privately confronting the individual concerned with the accusation. If that person repents and seeks the Lord for the right way forward to restore broken relationships and to set right those things that are wrong, then the sin is a matter between God and the individual and is not a public matter. This is the teaching of Jesus in Matthew 18. The Kansas City Fellowship acknowledged that they had been failing to use prophecy rightly in this regard as there had been occasions upon which prophetic revelation of individual sin had been spoken in the presence of the whole congregation without having first been spoken to the person concerned.

KCF have taken a public stand against such a misuse of prophecy and in this they are surely to be commended. But they are no doubt not the only church to have misused prophecy in this way. Even speaking "privately" about the sins of others can have a devastating effect upon the life of a fellowship. This kind of destructive gossiping can be given a pseudo-spiritual cover by claiming divine revelation of these wrong-doings. Even those who are in a right relationship with the Lord can sometimes drop into the sin of criticising brothers and sisters unjustly, or failing to go directly to them, or acting in a spirit of judgementalism. The Lord will find a way of rebuking and correcting us, either directly through speaking to us or through allowing things to go wrong in our lives that cause us to seek him for understanding. He may use others to speak to us if we are closed to receiving anything from him directly, as he used Nathan to speak to David.

There was an occasion in my own ministry when I was in danger of getting the prophetic message out of balance with too much emphasis upon impending judgement. I was in danger of losing sight of God's great love for his world, the creation of his own hands, and for all men and women whom he has made in his own image. The Lord spoke to me quite dramatically about his love and charged me to speak of it always even when bringing a warning of judgement.

We were jointly ministering in Switzerland to a conference of European leaders of Campus Crusade. We were out walking one afternoon when the Lord made it clear to me that he was going to speak to me with a special message which would come through an incident I would witness that afternoon, so I was extra alert to anything that might happen. An account of this incident has already been published in the book *Tell My People I Love Them*. It involved a little three-year-old girl who slid down the mountainside towards a precipice. Her father ran down the steep snow-covered slope and managed to save her just a few metres from the edge of the precipice with a two-hundred-foot drop onto rocks in the valley below. The Lord used this to speak to me about his great love for his people and his desire for the salvation of everyone. He said, "Did you see how that father did not hesitate to risk his own life for his child? That is how I love my people. Tell my people I love them!"

It was a lesson and a message I have never forgotten. Many times since then, when I have had a sleepless night, I have seen the look of terror in that little child's eyes and heard her screams as she slid helplessly towards certain death. I have often asked myself "If that child had been my own daughter would I have run down that steep snow-covered mountain slope?" I believe I would, although I can never know for sure. The one thing I do know is that I did not have sufficient love to risk my life for someone else's child. I was one of many people on that crowded mountain path that afternoon, but only one man leapt the guard rail and ran down the mountainside towards the precipice – the father of the child. God spoke to me powerfully that day about his fatherly love and gave me a command that I have never ceased to obey – Tell my people I love them!

I should not really have needed to be reminded of that message because the Lord had already spoken to me some years earlier, warning me to take great care in speaking about judgement. I was told never to do so except in the context of God's great love and his sorrow over the rebelliousness and sinfulness of his children. Once again God used a dramatic incident to convey his message. Our eldest daughter was less than three years old when she had to have spectacles. We were quite upset about this because of the restriction it put upon her in playing with other children. One day she fell while playing in the park. She grazed her hands, face and knees. I picked her up to comfort her and dust her down. While wiping away her tears I picked up her glasses and began to put them back on her face when she stopped me and through her sobs she said "I don't need my glasses when I cry. I can see your face quite clearly, Daddy". For some reason the tears corrected the myopia in her eyes and enabled her to focus correctly.

It was through this incident that God spoke to me, saying that if I wished to see his face clearly there had to be tears in my eyes – that it is only through brokenness that we can rightly approach the Lord.

The words of Psalm 51 took on a new meaning for me: "The sacrifices of God are a broken spirit; a broken and contrite heart, O God, you will not despise" (v.17). I was told never to speak about God's judgement except through tears.

Jeremiah is a prime example of a prophet who could never speak of the terrible things he saw coming upon the nation without weeping (cf Jeremiah 4:18–21) and Jesus himself wept over Jerusalem as he approached the city in the last days of his earthly life, knowing the judgement that would come upon it. The Lord's rebukes are always in love. When he needs to correct us and we see his face clearly we can see the sorrow in his eyes but when we return to him in repentance, the sorrow turns to joy. We can both testify to receiving the fulness of the Holy Spirit through an experience of brokenness.

Monica often remembers the loving rebuke she received from the Lord which transformed her perception of what he wanted to do through her life. She was a very shy private person who had difficulty in communicating in public. Although she was a teacher and was able to communicate well with children, she was not so easy with adults. She used to blush and stammer when people so much as looked at her and her mind would often go completely blank when she was expected to speak even in small groups. Marrying a minister was a traumatic experience as it threw her into the public eye which she never wanted, so she quickly settled into a supportive role and felt that this was the role that the Lord wanted for her. She believed that her ministry was "behind the scenes" as a back-up for me, and she justified this as all that the Lord required from her.

She could not believe that God would want, or even be able, to use her in any other way. It was

Ephesians 5:5-17

FOOTPRINTS

ONE night I had a dream—.

I dreamed I was walking along the beach with God and across the sky flashed scenes from my life. For each scene I noticed two sets of footprints in the sand, one belonged to me and the other to God.

When the last scene of my life flashed before us I looked back at the footprints in the sand. I noticed that at times along the path of life there was only one set of footprints.

I also noticed that it happened at the very lowest and saddest times of my life. This really bothered me and I questioned God about it. "God, you said that once I decided to follow you, you would walk with me all the way but I noticed that during the most troublesome times in my life there is only one set of footprints. I don't understand why in times when I needed you most, you would leave me."

God replied, "My precious, precious child, I love you and I would never, never leave you during your times of trials and suffering. When you see only one set of footprints it was then that I carried you."

ANON

Denzil J Reeves © 1986 Palm Tree Press

not until the Lord rebuked her, saying that her eyes were on herself rather than on him that she faced up to the situation. She realised that she was too concerned about how poorly she compared with others and what they thought of her. She eventually learned to take God at his word and to fix her eyes on the Lord. Then she realised how sinful she had been in limiting what God could do through her. Since then she has tried to be faithful in accepting that if he requires her to do something he will work through her and give her the power to do anything he asks. People who only know Monica now in a leadership capacity in an international ministry will probably find this quite surprising. But she still finds it difficult to talk about herself and what God has done in her life (and continues to do). This is probably the reason why most of the stories in this book are told from my standpoint!

c) Foretelling

There are occasions when God will speak to any of his servants personally giving revelation of the future. He will only show us what lies ahead when it is necessary for the working out of his purposes through our lives. Sometimes he speaks to us personally in forewarning. He does not want his servants to run into danger. Jesus taught his disciples to pray that God would lead them and guard them against temptation.

In biblical times, God often spoke to his servants giving them forewarning of impending danger. Paul had this experience when he was travelling to Jerusalem. He says that on the journey, in every town he visited, the Holy Spirit spoke to him and warned him that "prison and hardship" awaited him in Judea (Acts 20:23). Then in Caesarea, God sent the prophet Agabus to him with a specific warning: "He took Paul's belt, tied his own hands and feet with it and said, 'The Holy Spirit says, "In this way the Jews of Jerusalem will bind the owner of this belt and will hand him over to the Gentiles"'" (Acts 21:11).

God's purpose in giving the apostle this forewarning was to strengthen him for the hardship he was to endure and to assure him that it would actually be a part of God's purpose for his life which the Lord would wonderfully use for the concluding phase of his ministry. Had it not been for Paul's experience of imprisonment, there is no doubt that we would not have the letters he wrote from prison and some of the major teaching that forms a vital part of the New Testament. God fulfils his purposes in some strange ways but for those who have learned to listen to him as a regular part of their daily spiritual experience, the hardships do not come as a sudden shock that disturbs or even breaks their close walk with the Lord. God will usually give forewarning, but he will always prepare his servants so that they are able to stand and to stand firmly in the face of adversity and the onslaught of the enemy.

God does not always enable his servants to avoid problems – he is the Father who "did not spare his own Son but gave him up for us all" (Romans 8:32) – but he creatively uses testing times not only for our own character building and faith strengthening, but also for the carrying out of his purposes.

In 1988 we were ministering in Nigeria shortly after an outbreak of violence in the Northern province of Kaduna which had resulted in the martyrdom of many Christians. Some two hundred churches had been burnt down in communal riots inspired by extremist Muslims. There were many reports of the police failing to act to protect the Christians, but the outstanding feature of all the reports was of the Christians' refusal to retaliate. This made a deep impression upon the whole Muslim population. God had been preparing the Christians for that day for a long time. They were living in the predominantly Islamic northern region of Nigeria facing increasing pressures and mounting hostility from the Imams and Muslim fundamentalists.

When the day of persecution broke out the believers were ready and were enabled to stand firm by their complete trust in the Lord. Their witness, even in death, made such a powerful impression upon the whole region that when provincial elections were held some six months later, fourteen out of the nineteen elected State representatives were Christians including the Chairman. This astonished the whole nation and was seen as a powerful witness that was greatly glorifying to the name of the Lord Jesus. Large numbers of Muslims had voted for the Christians because they had demonstrated their complete trustworthiness.

There are many other reasons why God will give forewarning to his servants. Sometimes it is to enable them to be prepared to resist the attack of an enemy or even to take evasive action to avoid a confrontation. There was a period in the history of Israel when Elisha was given direct revelation of every impending attack from Syria. The King of Syria even suspected treason among his own staff because of the accuracy of the information that Elisha was passing on to Samaria. This enabled the army of Israel to be in the right place at the right time in order to repel each attack (2 Kings 6:8–12).

An example of forewarning for a different purpose occurred in Jerusalem shortly before the Jewish revolt of AD 68 that resulted in the Roman destruction of the city two years later and the slaughter of half-a-million Judean residents. The Christian community in Jerusalem were given revelation of these events through one of their prophets and the whole company of believers moved out of the trouble zone and settled at Pella where they were safe from attack and not one of them perished.

Demos Shakarian in *The Happiest People on Earth* tells how his own family escaped from Armenia to America as a result of divine revelation. A prophecy was given through a thirteen-year-old boy giving forewarning of the impending attack upon the Armenian population. The whole Pentecostal community received the word as a warning from the Lord and moved out before the mass slaughter of Armenians by the Turks.

We could give many other examples of God giving accurate information concerning the future to those exercising prophetic ministries. But there are dangers that also need to be noted. God is undoubtedly speaking to his servants in our own lifetime, and as the days become more violent, with the turmoil among the nations intensifying, we may expect to hear forewarnings of future danger more regularly. There are, however, many pitfalls for the unwary, the most obvious being that of the adulation of the prophet rather than the Lord who gives the prophetic message. But predictive prophecy itself can also be misused.

Paul Cain, who is linked with the Vineyard church, is one who often receives prophetic insight into the future. He is also well aware of the danger of people regarding him in some special way, rather than understanding the purpose for which prophecy is given, and giving all the glory to the Lord. On the first occasion of his meeting with John Wimber, Paul Cain told him that there would be an earthquake on the day he arrived in Anaheim and there would be another the day after he left. This prediction was accurately fulfilled and made a deep impression upon John Wimber, but he is careful to emphasise that there was a purpose for the Lord giving this information. It made him give special attention to the message Paul Cain was to bring to him concerning the problems in the leadership of the Vineyard church. This was not a message John Wimber wanted to hear, or was open to receive. But the Lord established the credibility of the prophetic messenger in such a way that the message could not be ignored.

The danger of accurately fulfilled prophecy being used to establish credibility lies in the fact that the one bringing the prophecy may become regarded as infallible, so that each time he brings a message it is received uncritically, and the instruction of the New Testament to test all prophecy is ignored. It is in this way that error and deception can get into the Church. This is a by-product of the adulation of men rather than God. The flesh all too easily gets in to confuse the work of God which is one of the current dangers facing us in the charismatic movement.

A further danger lies in our natural curiosity concerning the future. The whole world is playing games of predicting the future in all sorts of ways. Newspapers are full of speculation concerning political changes, and we are constantly bombarded with the results of opinion surveys and the latest forecast of cabinet reshuffles and government changes. The financial world plays its own games of gambling on the stock market and upon which currency will go up or down. Millions of dollars are gained and lost daily in these speculative enterprises. The world will gamble on anything – even the choice of an Archbishop to lead the Church of England! Betting was heavy on the two favourites, York and Liverpool, when suddenly in July 1990 money began to pour in upon an almost-unheard-of outsider – Bath and Wells – which no doubt precipitated the announcement of his appointment; probably to counter any charges of a leak of information!

The great danger facing the charismatic movement in handling the new emphasis on prophecy, is that of concentrating upon future prediction and losing sight of the basic biblical ministry of declaring the word of God for our times. There is something even more sinister than mere curiosity in the obsession of our generation with future prediction. The popularity of fortune telling and divination, and the fascination of horoscopes for millions of people today, is one of the results of the greater openness to the occult. One of our friends who is a teacher in London recounts his experience of facing a new class. The first question the children asked him was what his star sign was! The world is continually searching for paranormal experiences and supernatural knowledge and these desires can easily affect our judgement of prophecy in the Church if we do not strictly adhere to New Testament teaching.

A further danger is in the misuse of prophecy for manipulation by giving others what purports to be a word from the Lord for their lives. Directional prophecies of this kind can be particularly dangerous if they are not carefully weighed. They can even be manipulated in such a way as to become self-fulfilling prophecies.

There can be additional dangers if we are not aware of the necessity of waiting for the Lord to confirm his word concerning important decisions affecting our future.

> Even as a student I was aware of this and it stood me in good stead when a very nice girl from the Student Christian Union, whom I only knew casually, told me the Lord had spoken to her saying that we were to marry. I had sufficient sense to thank her for the great honour but to say it would be right to wait for the Lord to confirm it to me!

Ideally each of us should be hearing from the Lord for ourselves. If we learn to listen to him carefully, to maintain a right relationship with God and to be patient in handling the word he speaks to us, we will undoubtedly know the truth, for God does not wish us to be deceived and the Holy Spirit he has poured out upon us so abundantly is the Spirit of Truth.

d) Mission and Service

God also speaks personally to his servants in order to prepare them for mission and witness so that he can use them for the working out of his purposes.

This was Moses' experience when God called him to lead the Israelites out of slavery in Egypt. Moses protested "Who am I, that I should go to Pharaoh and bring the Israelites out of Egypt?" and God said, "I will be with you" (Exodus 3:11–12). Moses continued to make every kind of excuse and finally protested that he was not an eloquent speaker "I am slow of speech and tongue." Even God's offer "I will help you speak, and will teach you what to say" was not enough for Moses. He had not yet learned that God never gives a task without also giving the enabling. So in the end God arranged for his brother Aaron to be his mouthpiece "He will speak to the people for you, and it will be as if he were your mouth" (Exodus 4:10–17).

It is from this incident that we get our definition of "the prophet" as the "mouthpiece of God" since God himself referred to this arrangement in those terms. "See, I have made you like God to Pharaoh, and your brother Aaron will be your prophet. You are to say everything I command you and your brother Aaron is to tell Pharaoh" (Exodus 7:1–2). Once Moses had accepted God's commission, he no longer hesitated and was unflinching in his witness before Pharaoh. But even this was only a preparation for the even more demanding task of leading the people through forty years in the wilderness. Moses' prime responsibility throughout those years was to be the mouthpiece of God and to witness to the people.

Paul also had the experience of God breaking into his life dramatically and speaking to him personally to prepare him for his mission as "apostle to the Gentiles".

Each new phase of his ministry was directed by the Holy Spirit and at the turning points in his life God spoke clearly and directly to him. This happened when Paul and his companions were travelling in the region of Phrygia and Galatia and were expecting to continue visiting the churches of Asia Minor, when Paul had a vision of a man of Macedonia. He heard the man saying "Come over to Macedonia and help us" (Acts 16:9). It was this experience that proved to be a major milestone in fulfilling God's intention to take the Gospel to all the world and resulted in Paul crossing over to Greece and beginning the evangelisation of Europe.

Paul learned to trust the word he received from the Lord under all circumstances during his many years of hardship and facing danger through hundreds of miles of missionary activity. His absolute confidence in the Lord shows clearly in Luke's account of the storm and shipwreck en route to Rome. Although Paul was a prisoner, it was his witness that carried authority in the midst of the storm and saved a disaster in which all the lives of those on board could have been lost. Paul testified to the captain and crew of the ship that God had spoken to him and told him that not one of them would be lost "Only the ship will be destroyed . . . so keep up your courage, men, for I have faith in God that it will happen just as he told me" (Acts 27:21–25).

God still speaks personally today to prepare his servants for mission, and he will still today miraculously break into someone's life whom he wants to use for a special purpose. This was the experience of a Nigerian friend of ours, Solomon Lar, who is the Natural Ruler of the province of Jos and a former member of the Government of Nigeria. Following a military coup, he and many other politicians were arrested and imprisoned. During his imprisonment, a British missionary sent him a copy of *Prophecy Today* which made a deep impression upon him. He recalls how that one copy was passed around a thousand prisoners. He himself began to seek God in a new way and discovered that he too could hear from the Lord.

One of the men who was imprisoned with him was due to be executed in a few days, when Solomon got before the Lord on this man's behalf and was clearly told that God would intervene to save him. Solomon conveyed the message to him and prophesied that he would not die. The man was a Muslim but he was more than pleased to receive this message from a Christian. The days passed by and there was no reprieve sent from Lagos. He was due to be executed at dawn the following day, with Solomon still assuring him that the Lord had spoken and would be faithful to keep his word. During that night another military coup took place and the first act of the new rulers was to cancel all executions of political prisoners. The news reached the prison just a few hours before the man was due to die. To say that this experience created a deep impression upon him would be an understatement. He went to Solomon Lar and said "How did you know?" Solomon replied "The Lord Jesus told me". "I want to know this Jesus as my Lord", was the response and Solomon had the joy of leading him to Christ.

This man today has a powerful ministry of evangelism among Muslims travelling from place to place throughout Nigeria. All the prisoners knew what had happened and many of them came to faith through this dramatic incident. There is no more powerful demonstration of the prophetic word of God than the absolute faith of the prophet who receives a direct revelation and holds fast to the word until God fulfils it at the eleventh hour.

God loves to speak personally to his servants to use them to reach into the lives of those who do not know him, just as he used Solomon Lar to reach the condemned Muslim. God is wanting to speak to all his people but not all are listening. It often takes great courage to be obedient when

God speaks to us with a word for others.

This happened to a woman who had tried on numerous occasions to witness to her unbelieving neighbour but each time she had been firmly rebuffed. Then one day she clearly heard the Lord saying to her "Go to your neighbour and say 'It will be all right'". It seemed such a stupid message that she rejected it but the word came to her again later that morning. She argued with the Lord saying she could not possibly go to her neighbour with such a word. Eventually when she received the message a third time, she obeyed. She knocked on her neighbour's door and said "I have a message for you from God. He says 'It will be all right'". To her amazement instead of slamming the door in her face, her neighbour burst into tears and asked her to come in and talk to her. She had just that morning received a letter from the hospital confirming that she had cancer and had to go in for an operation. The word could not have been more timely and it enabled the believer for the first time to speak about the love of the Lord Jesus and to share Christ with her.

The prophetic word of the Lord is a most powerful tool for evangelism when used under the direction of the Holy Spirit and in the perfect timing of our God. We have believed for many years that God was going to raise up prophecy in the church to use it in evangelism. Prophecy and evangelism go together and we expect to see the prophet and the evangelist increasingly working more closely together. Prophecy prepares the way for the Gospel, just as John the Baptist went ahead of Jesus. The prophetic word of God often acts as a plough in breaking up the hard and fallow ground so that the good seed of the Gospel drops on fertile and prepared soil. This was what happened with the woman who witnessed to her neighbour. The prophetic word from the Lord broke through the neighbour's resistance and spoke to her of God's love and care in her time of need. The way was thus opened for the seed of the Gospel to take root and the believer was able to act as both prophet and evangelist.

The significant thing happening today is that God is using ordinary believers to receive prophetic revelation. The new prophetic movement of today is not controlled by the learned and the professional clergy. As Paul, one of the most learned men of his day, testified, God sometimes bypasses the wise man and the scholar. He asks "Has not God made foolish the wisdom of the wise? . . . For the foolishness of God is wiser than man's wisdom and the weakness of God is stronger than man's strength' (1 Corinthians 1:20–25). In the last days of the present age, as we see the prophecy of Joel coming to the climax of its fulfilment, we may expect to see an increase in God turning upside down the values of the world as he carries out his purposes.

There are good signs that many of the charismatic churches are waking up to the need for evangelism and for a greater involvement in social issues, both in the national scene and in the local community. Our fear is that many believers still prefer (or are encouraged) to concentrate upon receiving from God for themselves (personal needs, personal holiness) rather than upon being used in wider service in mission and witnessing to others.

e) Building Up and Encouraging

Paul says that "everyone who prophesies speaks to men for their strengthening, encouragement and comfort" (1 Corinthians 14:3). He also says that prophecy edifies the whole Church. This has always been the function of prophecy when God speaks to his servants. Even when bringing a rebuke it also has the effect of strenghthening their faith and encouraging them in the knowledge of the sovereignty of God. When our desire is to be in a right relationship with the Father we have no fear of his rebukes because we know that they are for our good and that God speaks in love. His perfect love casts out fear even when the message is unexpected or takes us by surprise.

This was Gideon's experience when he was threshing wheat down in the wine press hiding from the Midianite invaders. He was in this humiliating position, suffering from the dust choking his throat and blinding his eyes as he was beating out the corn in the confined space of the winepress instead of in the open air on the threshing floor, when God spoke to him. Through an angel Gideon was addressed as "Mighty Warrior". When Gideon protested, God spoke to him directly "Go in the strength you have and save Israel out of Midian's hand. Am I not sending you?" Following Gideon's further protest of his own weakness and inability, the Lord answered, "I will be with you" (Judges 6:11–16). God's purpose in speaking personally to Gideon was to convince him that the task he was being given could be accomplished, even though it could only be undertaken in God's way and in his strength. Gideon still needed convincing that he was rightly hearing from God. God always respects our desire for confirmation. He does not want us rushing ahead into ill-conceived actions that have not come from him. God was patient with Gideon in his requests for a confirming sign in the wet and dry fleeces.

There was an occasion in the life of Hezekiah when he fell sick at a critical period in the history of the nation when Jerusalem was still under threat from the Assyrians. Isaiah perceived that this was a terminal illness and sought to prepare the king for his death urging him to put his house in order. Hezekiah did not give up but prayed earnestly to the Lord to heal him. His prayer was heard. Then the word of the Lord came to Isaiah and he was told to go back and tell Hezekiah, "This is what the Lord, the God of your father David, says: I have heard your prayer and seen your tears; I will add fifteen years to your life. And I will deliver you and this city from the hand of the King of Assyria. I will defend this city" (Isaiah 38:4-6).

God spoke personally to Hezekiah through Isaiah to grant his request so that he could organise the defences of the city and lead his people effectively in the face of Sennacherib who had boasted in a letter to the king and in the hearing of the people of Jerusalem that their God would not be any more effective in protecting them than the gods of the other nations who had been conquered by the Assyrians. Hezekiah must have been enormously encouraged by God's granting of his request, and with his personal experience of miraculous healing, the level of his own faith must have increased to the point where he was able to serve the Lord by exercising prophetic and courageous leadership. "Be strong and courageous", he told the people. "Do not be afraid or discouraged because of the King of Assyria and the vast army with him, for there is a greater power with us than with him. With him is only the arm of flesh, but with us is the Lord our God to help us fight our battles." The Chronicler records that "The people gained confidence from what Hezekiah the king of Judah said" (2 Chronicles 32:7-8). When the Assyrians did attack, the faith in God of both king and people proved to be fully justified. "The Lord sent an angel, who annihilated all the fighting men and the leaders and officers in the camp of the Assyrian king. So he withdrew to his own land in disgrace" (2 Chronicles 32:21).

God sometimes speaks personally to his servants when they are in danger of giving up due to fierce opposition being encountered. This happened to Paul in Corinth. At the beginning of his mission there he concentrated upon reaching the Jews, preaching only in the synagogue. "Paul devoted himself exclusively to preaching, testifying to the Jews that Jesus was the Christ. But when the Jews opposed Paul and became abusive, he shook out his clothes in protest and said to them, 'Your blood be on your own heads! I am clear of my responsibility. From now on I will go to the Gentiles'" (Acts 18:5–6). The Lord spoke personally to Paul to stop him leaving Corinth and to encourage him to continue witnessing to the Jews as well as the Gentiles. In a vision one night, God said "Do not be afraid; keep on speaking, do not be silent. For I am with you, and no one is going to attack and harm you, because I have many people in this city" (v. 10). Paul stayed there a further eighteen months with the result that a strong church was founded in Corinth and also there were a number of notable conversions in the Jewish community, including two of the "rulers of the synagogue" – Crispus and Sosthenes and their households.

God still speaks today to encourage and strengthen his servants, particularly when they are facing difficult times of opposition that might deflect them from the path of ministry that the Lord wants them to follow. This was our experience recently when an unknown minister telephoned from South Africa to our ministry base in London, saying that the Lord had given him a message and told him to call. He gave me a personal message that brought the whole Team great encouragement. It spoke clearly into the situation we were facing in the ministry at a time when we were feeling discouraged and weak. The message included a word of knowledge that enabled us to understand the situation more clearly. The message also gave us a fresh direction for the ministry that we were feeling after but were awaiting confirmation before taking any decisive steps. We knew this to be a word from the Lord because it concerned things he had already been saying to us and no one outside our ministry team would have known. It also had the effect of increasing our faith and strengthening us, which is one of the tests of this kind of prophecy.

This man subsequently visited London and brought personal words of encouragement to a number of members of our Team at a time when we were considering the whole role of personal prophecy within the Church.

Using Personal Prophecy

There is a strong emphasis upon personal prophecy in the Pentecostal and charismatic churches today. At its simplest level this kind of prophecy is what Mike Bickle describes in Kansas City Fellowship teaching notes as "thoughts or ideas that God brings to mind". He says that "these may well include words of knowledge while praying for someone" which are given to enable more effective ministry. In KCF, everyone is encouraged to seek to prophesy in this way as it is considered the safest form of prophecy which Bickle describes as "Level 1" in the four levels of prophecy he recognises. According to KCF teaching, Levels 2, 3 and 4 are achieved through constant practice which increases proficiency and accuracy. In the higher levels "prophets" are permitted to prophesy in other dimensions and beyond the local fellowship with more notice being taken of their words. It is interesting to note that they do not feel they have any Level 4 prophets at present who can speak directly to the nation.

But, even in the simple first level of prophecy there are dangers if the words are accepted uncritically. Mike Bickle does say that all prophetic revelation must be tested. But the practice of including words of knowledge alongside prophecy increases the difficulty of testing prophecy. Words of knowledge have the effect of lowering the guard of the one receiving ministry because it is clearly supernatural. When it is immediately followed by a prophecy, the tendency is to accept both the word and message as coming from God. The word of knowledge, although it is true, may have come from a spirit other than the Holy Spirit in which case the prophecy also may be false in its origin.

Prophetic revelation given by one person to another is never easy to weigh instantly and puts the person being ministered to under pressure to accept it as part of the ministry being offered. Because of the personal nature of the message being given, a personal response is called for in a way that does not apply if the prophecy is given to the whole Church or is one for the nation. This pressure is increased where the words "Thus says the Lord" or similar phrases are used because it leaves no option other than acceptance or rejection. If God really is saying this, it must be accepted. There can be no argument or acceptance in part. It is either right or wrong. Even in small group settings or on a personal level, prophecy can be misused for manipulating the lives of others even though the one giving the prophecy may not be aware of this.

It would be much better if those who are ministering to others on a personal level would speak in the third person rather than the august "first person singular", and say something like, "I believe the Lord is bringing into my mind a scripture for you that should speak to your need." This would not only have the effect of showing a little more humility on the part of the one ministering, but also have the great benefit of directing attention to the word of God in the Bible. The more people can be encouraged to study scripture and to be familiar with the word of God and apply it to their own edification and upbuilding, the more the whole Church will be built up in the faith and established on a firm foundation. This is the only sure way that prophecy can become established in the churches without danger of the intrusion of occultic influences and deception.

Chapter Five

The God Who Works in Power

Throughout the Bible God is shown to be a God of power, but he is not a God who acts capriciously like the gods of the pagan nations. He is shown to be the Creator of the world and of the whole universe which he has set in order and which functions according to rules that he, himself, designed. The natural order of things can be trusted and so can the God of creation. Just as we know that the sun will rise in the morning, so we know that God will not deny himself. There are, however, certain circumstances under which God will intervene in the rules governing the natural order of creation in order to fulfil his purposes as when he held back the waters of the Red Sea. But he will never act against the fundamental attributes of his own nature. Having revealed certain aspects of his nature such as his faithfulness, his justice, his love and his mercy he will always act in such a way as will conform to these eternal qualities. It was this dependability of God that enabled the prophets to prophesy. They knew that once God had revealed his word to them, he would undoubtedly fulfil it so that they could declare it with confidence to the whole world – whether believers or unbelievers.

It was this confidence in God that enabled Moses to go to Pharaoh with the demand from the Lord "Let my people go!" (Exodus 6:4–12). Moses knew that God not only could, but *would*, back up his word with his deeds. When Pharaoh, who had at last released the Israelites from slavery, changed his mind and sent the army to recapture them, Moses was forewarned. God had already told him what would happen and that he would do something that would "gain glory" for himself "through Pharaoh and all his army so that the Egyptians would know that he was God" (Exodus 14:4). In fact it was not only the Egyptians but all the surrounding nations who heard of the mighty miracle of the crossing of the Red Sea. We find Rahab, the prostitute in Jericho, referring to this some forty years later "We have heard how the Lord dried up the water of the Red Sea for you when you came out of Egypt . . . Our hearts sank and everyone's courage failed because of you, for the Lord your God is God in heaven above and on the earth below" (Joshua 2:10–11).

Moses was already confident that God was not only a God of power but also a God of his word, but it must have been a tremendous test of his faith when the Egyptian chariots bore down upon them. With the enemy behind them and the waters of the Red Sea ahead of them, to human eyes the position appeared hopeless. But it is in this situation that we find Moses addressing the people confidently, "Do not be afraid. Stand firm and you will see the deliverance the Lord will bring you today . . . The Lord will fight for you, you need only to be still" (Exodus 14:13–14).

At this stage, Moses still did not know what action God would take, so immediately after strengthening the people we find him crying out to the Lord. God rebuked him "Why are you crying out to me? Tell the Israelites to move on. Raise your staff and stretch out your hand over the sea . . ." (Exodus 14:15–16). God demonstrated his power even over the forces of nature that he himself had created. Clearly God, who always revealed himself as a God of order, would only do such a thing in the most exceptional circumstances and for an explicit reason.

The exceptional circumstances were the saving of the whole nation whom he had called into a covenant relationship with himself for the purpose of using them to reveal himself to the whole world. Clearly, for his own name's sake, he could not allow them to be destroyed. His act of salvation in bringing them out of Egypt achieved many things. It showed his own people that he is a God who hears the cries of his people, who has compassion upon them, and that he is a God who saves. It also demonstrated his power over the whole of nature, his faithfulness to keep his word and through all this God gained glory to his name not only among his own people but also in the unbelieving nations.

It was because of the spiritual significance of the crossing of the Red Sea for understanding the very nature and purposes of God, that the prophets of Israel referred to it time after time throughout the history of the nation. It was not just a focal point in history but a demonstration by God of fundamental aspects of his own nature. He is a God of power but he will only use that power for his own glory and for the fulfilment of his own purposes. He cannot be persuaded to act against his own will.

Power Today

It is important to understand these basic biblical principles in relation to the power of God when giving consideration to what is popularly known today as God's action in "signs and wonders". God has already established the ground rules. They are perfectly clear in scripture and there are no indications to encourage us to believe that he will change them at any period in history

– not even in the last days.

We cannot find any biblical justification for the "New Breed" teaching of extra power to believers in the last days, propagated by the Anaheim/KCF Ministry. The essence of this teaching is that God will give extraordinary power to believers in the closing period of this age, who will be the final generation, who will witness the return of Jesus and who will form the Bride of Christ. KCF teach that this generation began with those born since 1973 and that we are already witnessing the outpouring of the Spirit upon believers in a new way, particularly upon the believing parents of the final generation who have the obligation to prepare their children for the very special purpose that God has for them.

According to this teaching the "New Breed" has already emerged and God is giving supernatural power to those who are prepared to take a stand for the Lord. As they do so they will find an increase in the spiritual power available to them. They will stretch out their hands and perform extraordinary deeds that will astound the unbelievers and will overcome the opposition of those who are enemies of the Gospel. They will be given power to subdue even the secular authorities in the nations who will not submit to God.

The expectation of this teaching is that the final generation will be used by God to prepare the way for the Second Coming of Christ. God will not only give them authority over the Church, but he will place the government of the nations upon their shoulders in readiness for Christ to claim his Kingdom.

This teaching is very similar to the beliefs that were taught in some of the Pentecostal churches in the 1940s which became known as "Latter Rain" teaching. It also goes under the title of "Dominion Theology". In part, it is probably a reaction against an over-emphasis in some churches upon the expectation of the Rapture, whereby all the true believers will be lifted up out of the world before what is known as the "Great Tribulation" occurs. Many Christians were using this belief as an excuse for opting out of any responsibility for the current state of the world or for any form of Christian action or participation in political or social affairs. One Christian leader, reacting against this kind of Rapture-based-negativism, said he did not want to be found simply standing around the bus-stop waiting for the Lord to come along. He wanted to be involved in the action leading up to Christ's return.

Attractive as it may sound to believe that our generation is favoured by God with extraordinary spiritual gifts enabling us to perform miraculous signs and wonders that will dazzle the world, this is more akin to Hollywood type "Superman" fantasy films than the teaching of the New Testament. The prophecy of Joel does indeed refer to the "last days" as being the time when God would abundantly pour out his Spirit upon all the believers regardless of their worldly status, but as we have already pointed out, the period of the last days began at Pentecost and there is certainly nothing in the New Testament to suggest that those who are alive at the end of the period will be more favoured than those in the first generation – the apostolic age. The apostles themselves performed many signs and wonders but they did not perform the kind of supernatural exploits being foretold in the "prophecies" of some of the KCF preachers.

These prophecies are of course very popular with many people. They are the very things that people want to hear. Many of the more recent songs in the charismatic movement focus upon "power" and reflect the desire for increased power to be given to us. These songs cause us some anxiety because they can so easily become the desires of the flesh where power is wanted for the wrong reasons. All the systems of the world are based upon power of one form or another – economic, political or military.

The teaching of Jesus is that his kingdom is not of this world and his followers are not to look for power in the same way as the world does. The disciples were not to "lord it over" others or "exercise authority" in the same way as unbelievers (Matthew 20:25–28). Believers are to seek first the kingdom of God and his righteousness, and then all the material things that we need will be added to us. The kingdom to which Jesus refers consists in right relationships, first with God and then with others. These right relationships are established in peace, and not in power, and through the Lord Jesus who gives his peace "not as the world gives" (John 14:27).

Peter dealt decisively with Simon the sorcerer, who tried to buy the power of the Holy Spirit when he saw that it was given when the apostles laid their hands upon believers in Samaria and prayed for them. Peter told him "You have no part or share in this ministry because your heart is not right before God". This man had supposedly turned away from the occultic practices of his past when he had been converted under the ministry of Philip the evangelist and had been baptised. Peter saw that his motives for wanting the power of the Holy Spirit were not right, even though he said he wanted it so that those upon whom he laid his hands would receive the Spirit of God. Simon had actually been regarded by many people in Samaria as divine, because of the power he exercised through his magic, and Peter discerned that he would misuse the gift of the Holy Spirit in the same way as he had used his magic to manipulate the lives of others and bring them into submission to his will.

This is the grave danger of any kind of occultic influence in the lives of those exercising spiritual gifts, and particularly those claiming to receive prophetic revelation. Even if they have long since repented of their involvement in sorcery and witchcraft or any other form of occultism, these spiritual forces of evil can still have a subtle influence often without the person being aware of them. The occultic sins go the deepest, they touch the very depths of spiritual nature in a human being, and you can never be completely sure that there is are no after-effects. The repentant sinner who comes to Christ renouncing occultic practices should be assured of complete salvation, total forgiveness and cleansing through the blood of Christ but this does not automatically mean that all forms of ministry are then open to that person. Simon the sorcerer was probably totally sincere in desiring to be able to minister to others, so that they could receive the Holy Spirit, but Peter perceived something wrong and rebuked him. To his credit, the man immediately responded in repentance, but there is no evidence that Peter changed his mind and granted his request for the power he longed to possess.

Jesus also refused the request for ministry involvement of a man whom he had just delivered from demonic possession. Before his healing the man confessed to the name of "Legion" because of the many demons in his life. After Jesus had cast them out, Luke records "The man from whom the demons had gone out begged to go with him, but Jesus sent him away, saying, "'Return home and tell how much God has done for you'" (Luke 8:38–39). This man wanted to be fully involved in ministry with Jesus but he would not permit him to be one of his close disciples sharing in the ministry with him. He told him that he should stay in his home town where there was important ministry for him to do as a witness to all that God had done for him.

God is able, without doubt, to forgive, cleanse and heal completely anyone who has been deeply involved in the occult but it is nevertheless dangerous for them *ever* to engage in any form of ministry exercising divine revelation. This does not mean that they cannot minister to others; indeed they may have a very effective ministry to others with similar backgrounds, testifying to their own deliverance and bringing others to a saving knowledge of Christ. But prophecy carries enormous responsibility for good or for harm because it is dealing not with the words or opinions of men, but with what God is saying. We cannot be too careful in guarding the church against deception especially in regard to the exercise of prophetic gifts and ministry.

> My major hesitation in regard to the Kansas City prophets, during my visit to KCF in December 1989, was that I discerned an occultic influence. I shared this with John Wimber, Mike Bickle and Paul Cain when I met with them in London in July 1990, and they agreed with me that my discernment had been correct. It was a situation of which they were aware and with which they were attempting to deal.

Derek Prince issued a statement in the same month saying that he had preached at Kansas City Fellowship in March 1990 and had discerned an occultic influence to which he referred at the time.

However spiritually gifted a person may appear to be in receiving a multitude of visions, out-of-body experiences, words of revelation or accurate words of knowledge, it is very dangerous to place reliance upon these supernatural phenomena and allow them to give credibility to the one exercising ministry. Surely the words of Jesus warn us against this kind of gullibility. Jesus said categorically, "Many will say to me on that day, 'Lord, Lord, did we not prophesy in your name, and in your name drive out demons and perform many miracles?' Then I will tell them plainly,' I never knew you. Away from me, you evildoers!'" (Matthew 7:21–23). Jesus was specifically warning about the danger posed to the church by false prophets and he was referring here to people who not only claimed to be ministering in his name but *actually believed* they were doing so. They spoke to him *face to face* saying that they had prophesied in his name and performed miracles in his name but he still stated that he did not know them. Why? The answer has to be that they were ministering in the wrong spirit, probably without even being aware that they were doing so. Jesus does not say whether they were ministering in their own *human spirit* or were driven by an *evil spirit* but one thing is certain – they were not empowered by the *Holy Spirit*.

Expressions of Power

Signs and wonders should not be regarded as evidence of the power of the Holy Spirit. The enemy is an expert at counterfeiting all these signs as Moses found out when he confronted Pharaoh. "Moses and Aaron went to Pharaoh and did just as the Lord commanded. Aaron threw his staff down in front of Pharaoh and his officials, and it became a snake. Pharaoh summoned the wise men and sorcerers, and the Egyptian magicians also did the same things by their secret arts: each one threw down his staff and it became a snake" (Exodus 7:10–12). It is worth noting that although Aaron's staff swallowed up the others, Pharaoh's heart became hard and he would not listen to God's messengers.

It was no doubt for this same reason that Jesus consistently refused the Pharisees' request for a sign to prove that he was the Messiah. Jesus knew that miraculous signs prove nothing. He told them that no sign would be given to them except the "sign of Jonah" (Matthew 16:4), which was a reference to his own death and resurrection after three days, but was no doubt also a reference to the message of repentance that Jonah was commissioned to take to Ninevah. Jesus did, in fact, do many miraculous signs during his ministry but John notes that they were ineffective in convincing the leaders of

111

his divine sonship: "Even after Jesus had done all these miraculous signs in their presence, they still would not believe in him" (John 12:37).

It is wrong to expect signs and wonders to bring people into the Kingdom. Jesus, himself refused to use his miraculous powers for such a purpose. He said, "If they do not listen to Moses and the Prophets, they will not be convinced even if someone rises from the dead" (Luke 16:31). Jesus taught his disciples that signs and wonders *follow* the preaching of the Word of God. When they do this the miracles bring glory to God, which should be the case in every demonstration of his power. It is the flesh that desires the *excitement* of signs and wonders. Just as the crowds followed Jesus "for the loaves" so today the crowds will still run after him for spiritual entertainment.

God is working in power today through a fresh outpouring of the Holy Spirit. We have already noted that this fresh outpouring is of quantity rather than quality. Millions of believers today are receiving the Holy Spirit and are open to the exercise of spiritual gifts which is transforming the scene in many churches. The great spiritual awakening, that is a characteristic of today, is bringing vast numbers of new believers into the Kingdom. Recently a thousand new converts were baptised in a mass baptism in Korea. We ourselves have spoken at a church in Surabaya, Indonesia, which has grown from nothing to more than twenty-five thousand members in less than ten years. The remarkable thing about this church is that it is planted in a predominantly Muslim area. We have seen the rows of new believers awaiting baptism every Sunday. In order to cope with the increasing numbers, this church now baptises every Wednesday as well as Sundays.

It is, however, not simply the vast numbers of new believers coming into the Kingdom in our day which is the most significant characteristic. It is also the openness to the Holy Spirit and the exercise of the spiritual gifts which is transforming the whole church scene. There are many churches today led by a multiple leadership team in contrast to the old one-man-band type of ministry where the pastor was expected to take the lead in every aspect of the life of the congregation and even oversee its administration regardless of his gifting.

But this does not mean to say that churches are now adopting a New Testament pattern of leadership with a right blending of the five-fold ministries to which Paul refers in Ephesians 4 – apostles, prophets, evangelists, pastors and teachers. Paul says that these ministries are given by God "to prepare God's people for works of service, so that the body of Christ may be built up" (4:12). Churches today may be using the leadership team simply to duplicate the one-man-band ministry, or at best to divide up that task between them, sharing the load of pastoral care and administration.

But the reason God has given different ministry gifts is for a blending of the gifts in such a way that the whole body grows to spiritual maturity. It is only when the different ministry gifts are recognised as essential for growth to maturity, that they will be practised in the churches. There needs to be a recognition of the essential place within the fellowship of each of the ministries of prophecy, evangelism, pastoral care and teaching as well as the pioneering role of apostolic leadership. Currently pastoral care takes precedence over everything, although teaching increasingly occupies a place in many churches. But the other ministries are rarely exercised in local churches. Even the ministry of evangelism has largely been pushed out of the church into para-church organisations. These ministry gifts do not have to be exercised by full-time theologically and professionally trained clergy in each local church. Perhaps one of the greatest needs of the Church is to revise our whole understanding of ordination and bring it into line with New Testament teaching.

The Church has for centuries recognised differences in gifting for use among the laity, such as the gifts referred to in Romans 12 which include serving or administration, giving generously and helping others. These practical gifts have always been encouraged in the local church which could hardly function without them.

The new thing that is happening today is the recognition of the gifts in 1 Corinthians 12, which include three groups – messages of wisdom and knowledge; gifts of faith, healing, miraculous powers, prophecy and distinguishing between spirits; and speaking in tongues and interpretation. There are many churches where some of these gifts are being regularly exercised and others that are seeking to use all of them. These gifts are not regarded as the prerogative of professionally trained ministers but may be exercised by any Spirit-filled Christians. The barriers between clergy and laity are slowly coming down in those churches where there is growing confidence in the exercise of spiritual gifts, but most churches have a long way to go before there is a right balance and blending of ministry gifts, spiritual gifts and natural giftings.

Where all the gifts are being rightly exercised the power of God will be seen to be at work in the regular life of the fellowship just as it was in the early days of the New Testament churches. Extra-ordinary happenings were ordinary everyday occurrences. Luke records that "people brought the sick into the streets and laid them on beds and mats so that at least Peter's shadow might fall on some of them as he passed by. Crowds gathered also from the towns around Jerusalem bringing their sick and those tormented by evil spirits, and all of them were healed" (Acts 5:15–16). The power of God was clearly seen in signs and wonders as the disciples carried out the command of the Lord to be witnesses to his resurrection and to all that he had taught and done during his earthly ministry. As they faithfully proclaimed the word of God, so the power of God fell upon the people.

But the Church very soon had to face up to the problems generated by signs and wonders being performed in the presence of unbelievers and not simply in the company of believers. Paul and Barnabas had a traumatic experience in Lystra that nearly cost Paul his life when they healed a man who had been lame from birth. The crowds didn't understand the right exercise of spiritual gifts, neither were they prepared to give the glory to the God they did not know, rather they shouted "The gods have come down to us in human form" and they tried to deify Paul and Barnabas. When the apostles refused to accept the worship of men, the mood changed to violent hostility (Acts 14:8–20).

There are four basic biblical principles for the right exercise of spiritual power noted in *Rich Christians, Poor Christians* (Monica Hill; Marshall Pickering 1989, pp.112–13). The first is the recognition of our own **powerlessness**, that it is only God who has the power to heal or to perform miracles and that he works through our weakness. Secondly, God's power must always **glorify God** and not man. Thirdly, the power of God in signs and wonders is given **to believers** for believers and not for unbelievers, it is not intended to be used for evangelism. And fourthly that signs and wonders **follow** rather than precede the preaching of the Gospel.

The right use of the spiritual gifts should naturally fulfil these four basic principles, and there will often be a blending of spiritual gifts that will release the power of God to deal with a particular situation. This is often seen in miraculous healing. Healings are among the most common occurrences today in churches where the spiritual gifts are recognised and there are multitudes of believers throughout the world today who could testify to the healing power of God over their physical infirmities.

At a recent conference led by the PWM Team one of

the leaders received a word of knowledge during a time of worship. He said the Lord was showing him that there was someone present suffering from a disorder of the colon and God was saying that he was going to heal it that day. A woman jumped to her feet and immediately came to the front with eager expectation as the description accurately fitted her condition which was unknown to the speaker and most of those in the hall. She had suffered from this physical problem that had affected her digestive system for many years, and surgery and medical treatment had all proved ineffective. The leaders gathered around her, laid on hands and prayed. She experienced an immediate relief and her joy was shared by the whole company. From that time her whole life has changed through being able to eat normally for the first time for years. When miracles of healing such as this occur, it encourages the whole body of believers, it increases faith and causes them to glorify God.

Supernatural powers can, however, be misused. It was probably because Jesus was well aware of this, that he usually tried to keep his most spectacular healing miracles out of the public eye. When Jesus healed a man with leprosy, Matthew notes that he told him "See that you don't tell anyone" (8:4), and when he restored the sight of two blind men in response to their faith he "warned them sternly, 'See that no one knows about this'" (Matthew 9:30). Mark also notes that when Jesus healed many sick people he warned them not to tell others. The warning was particularly severe to the parents of the little twelve-year-old girl whom he raised from the dead (Mark 5:43).

Jesus was equally careful to conceal supernatural revelation, as when Peter recognised him as the Christ. Jesus acknowledged "This was not revealed to you by man, but by my Father in heaven . . . Then he warned his disciples not to tell anyone that he was the Christ" (Matthew 16:13–20). When others similarly perceived him to be Messiah, he warned them not to tell others who he was (Matthew 12:16). Jesus was continually turning people's eyes to the Father and not to himself. For this reason he did not even want his Messiahship recognised until the right timing of the Father. He certainly did not wish to be followed by crowds who were simply interested in his miraculous powers and were looking for the excitement of the supernatural.

There is grave danger today in the exercise of spiritual gifts if we do not keep firmly in mind the basic biblical principles for their right handling. There are also important lessons to be learnt from the way Jesus showed total obedience to the Father, and the care with which he avoided drawing to himself the adulation of the crowds, or using his miraculous powers to convince them of the genuineness of the ministry he had been sent by the Father to accomplish. The temptation facing anyone in ministry is to use their supernatural gifting as a means of establishing their ministry or convincing others of their credibility. Jesus himself rejected this temptation at the very beginning of his ministry, when he refused the Devil's invitation to throw himself off the pinnacle of the temple and demonstrate the miraculous power he had by saving himself in front of all the people in Jerusalem.

The large charismatic conferences and celebrations today can easily become arenas of entertainment. They can offer great opportunity to those in ministry to draw the adulation of the crowds, especially where there is an expectation among those present of God revealing his presence through miraculous deeds. Words of knowledge, prophecy, gifts of healings and miracles can all be misused in this way. When the supernatural gifts are being used in the presence of a large crowd, this creates an uncritical atmosphere. Words that would be carefully tested if spoken in a small group, are allowed to pass unchallenged because there is often no opportunity for weighing prophecy or confirming words of knowledge under these circumstances. Crowd behaviour is always different from individual or small group behaviour and it is not difficult for any experienced speaker to work on the emotions of a large crowd until their critical faculties are dimmed. People rarely stop to consider the fact that occultists can duplicate most of these things, and it is for this reason that New Testament teachers insist on testing everything in the realm of prophetic revelation.

Use of Words of Knowledge

The Church of England Newspaper carried a front page report of the July 1990 meetings at Holy Trinity, Brompton led by John Wimber and the Anaheim/KCF team. The report particularly focused on the ministry exercised by Paul Cain. It spoke disparagingly of his preaching saying most people were bored, but it noted a sudden change in the atmosphere when he reached into his pocket and drew out a handful of cards and began reading messages that he claimed to have received from God before the meeting during a time of prayer. The messages were for named individuals and each began with a word of knowledge concerning that person that served to establish the credibility for the prophetic word that followed. The CEN report indicated that this was what the people were waiting for and they were greatly impressed at the accuracy of the words to some of the well-known leaders. Paul Cain himself referred to the fact that in the early days of his ministry this used to be regarded as a legitimate form of entertainment among the Pentecostal congregations whose members did not have television and were forbidden to visit cinemas or engage in other forms of secular entertainment.

This form of personal prophecy is not really as spectacular as sometimes appears. Most ministry teams visiting an area, or speaking to a conference outside their own home base, would be given a list of participants registered for the conference or of supporting churches. It would not be unusual for the organisers to indicate the names of those with leadership responsibilities in the area so that they could be prayed for by the team as part of their preparation for ministry. In our own Ministry Team we would normally expect this to happen and in our team meetings we pray for the leaders by name. It is not at all unusual for one or other of the team to receive a word for one or more of the leaders. We believe, however, it is a much wiser practice to ensure that these words are given privately. When words of knowledge and prophecies are given in a large public meeting, it can easily come to be regarded as a public display that brings glory to those who are ministering rather than glory to God.

We would like to make it clear that we are not accusing Paul Cain of such a sin. We believe him to be a man of humility who would not deliberately seek personal adulation. But to organise meetings of this character, where he is expected to come onto the stage at a certain point and exercise this kind of ministry, is particularly dangerous. It can easily lead to the expectation of a supernatural performance as part of the spiritual entertainment of the evening.

Our concern is with the right exercising of spiritual gifts so that the Church is guarded against deception. We believe the only way this is possible is by adhering strictly to New Testament teaching and practice. If words of knowledge and personal prophecy for well-known leaders are given in public there is a danger of their being uncritically accepted by the crowd, which puts additional pressure on those who are the subject of the prophecy, even if they themselves try to weigh the revelation given. Usually there is no chance of doing this at the time, and certainly no opportunity for telling all those present whether or not it is accepted as a word from the Lord.

We would also like to make it clear that we are not suggesting that words of knowledge do not have a legitimate part to play in ministry. Indeed it is one of the major characteristics of our day that God is giving prophetic revelation as an essential part of the right exercise of spiritual gifts and ministries. When God acts in power, he usually reveals to his servants something of his intention because this not only increases faith but actually gives us the knowledge of what to pray for, or of how to minister to meet the real needs of others.

All those exercising a ministry of pastoral counselling should seek for God to reveal to them the real needs of those to whom they are ministering. This enables them to pray about the real issues, not simply those reported to them, and to offer wise counsel as directed by the Holy Spirit. It is not always necessary to speak out loud, in the form of "a word of knowledge", what God reveals to us. When God gives such a word, it is for a purpose and sometimes it is better simply to "pray with knowledge" rather than to "crush" or humiliate the person receiving ministry with a devastating word – especially if there are others present who would hear the word. On other occasions it is essential to speak out the word in order to minister effectively.

On one occasion, our Ministry Team was speaking at a large meeting in the Pavilion, Bath. It had been a long meeting with a number of conversions, others were filled with the Holy Spirit and there were many demonstrations of the power of God to heal. It was difficult to close the meeting. People simply did not want to go home because the presence of the Lord was so real. It was past midnight when the last people were making their way out of the hall. A tall man was standing by the door as I approached. He stepped forward and said "Would you mind just praying for me, as I have a terrible headache". I followed my usual practice and simply rested my hand on the man's shoulder and asked the Lord to show me how I should pray. The Lord said to me "Tell this man to open his eyes and look at you, then say one word 'Freemansonry'".

I did exactly as I was told, and as I spoke the word the man's knees buckled and he began to shake and said, "How did you know?" I said, "I don't even know your name and I know nothing about you. The only way I could have known is because the Lord has revealed it to me." The man told me that he had left the Freemasons three years earlier, so I asked him if he had ever formally renounced the vows he had made at his initiation. He said that he hadn't. I said, "If you really want to be clear, that is what you must do." He said that he did, so I made up a form of words for him to repeat after me renouncing the vows he had sworn when becoming a Freemason and reaffirming his commitment to the Lord Jesus Christ. I then prayed for him and laid on hands and asked the Holy Spirit to come upon him. He immediately fell to the floor and a few moments later sat up praising God in tongues, filled with a new found joy and peace. I never did pray for his headache!

On another occasion, our team was in Eastbourne leading a five-day mission at the Town Hall. At the close of the final meeting many people came forward for ministry and I could see an elderly woman with a white stick being led to the front. I found myself hoping she would be taken to one of the other leaders or members of the team and not be brought to me as I was very tired at the end of a demanding period of ministry. The young woman leading her guided her straight to me and I asked her what she was seeking. She said she wanted her sight and when she told me that she had been totally blind for ten years and could not even distinguish between night and day, I knew I simply did not have the faith to pray for her sight to be restored. I lifted her to the Lord, as is my usual practice, and asked him what to do. To my amazement I heard him clearly say "I will heal her". I said, "Lord, I cannot pray for that", and he said, "Ask me, and you will see my power to restore her sight".

Quite suddenly my tiredness was gone and was replaced by the excitement of great expectation. I knew that God was going to heal this woman and so I was able to pray believing. To my astonishment, after I had prayed she said she still couldn't see, so I asked the Lord again what I should do and he said that I was to send her away, believing that she was already healed and that her sight would slowly be restored.

I had already seen this happen with others whose sight had been restored from complete blindness, so I did exactly as I was bidden. I told her that the Lord had promised that her sight would be restored and that she was to go on her way rejoicing, knowing that God is faithful and he would keep his word. Although this woman was more than seventy years of age she had only been a believer about three months and her faith was like that of an eager child.

She was taken back to the Old People's Home where she lived and the young woman who accompanied her told the matron what had happened. Already the blind woman was saying she could see light as she had entered the building. The matron took her into the lounge and put on a number of lights and asked her to count them. She did so accurately, pointing to each one and there was great rejoicing and praising of God.

These two little stories each illustrate an important biblical principle in handling the prophetic word of God. The Lord gives us revelation knowledge for a special purpose to enable us to know how to minister, particularly to those who don't know what their real needs are, as in the case of the man complaining of headaches. The Lord will also speak to us directly to enable us to pray in faith in a way that we could not if we had not got the assurance of knowing that we were praying for something that he had already promised he would do. This gives us the confidence to be able to pray for those things that would otherwise appear impossible.

These principles are to be seen in many incidents recorded in scripture but none more clearly than when Elijah encountered the prophets of Baal on Mount Carmel. This in itself was a tremendous victory of faith for the prophet but his work was not completed until the rain fell to break the drought which he had prayed in three-and-a-half years before. God had told him before the contest on Carmel, "Go and present yourself to Ahab, and I will send rain on the land" (1 Kings 18:1).

Elijah knew that once the land had been cleansed from the false prophets of Baal and Asherah, God would fulfil his promise. He then told Ahab that the rain was about to come and that he should leave the mountain and go home. Elijah began to pray for the rain. Seven times he sent his servant to look out towards the Mediterranean and eventually the man reported "a cloud as small as a man's hand is rising from the sea", and shortly afterwards "the sky grew black with clouds, the wind rose, a heavy rain came on" (1 Kings 18: 44–45).

There are four stages in the fulfilment of the word of God to be seen in this account of the miracle of Mount Carmel.

1. The prophetic revelation was given to Elijah of what God intended to do.

2. The prophet declared it by faith as the word of God.
3. Elijah prayed for God to fulfil his promise.
4. The God who works in power acted according to his word.

This is the model for those who wish to follow biblical principles in the right handling of spiritual gifts. The first essential is to hear from God. Without this divine revelation, you cannot be sure that you are praying in accordance with the will of the Father. Once you have heard from him, you can then have the faith both to declare the word to others and to pray believing. It is this quality of believing prayer based on the certainty of the Father's intentions to fulfil his word that releases divine power.

Chapter Six

The God Who Declares His Truth

If we are right in discerning a fresh move of God today then it will be a declaration of truth. For God is truth and the word of God is truth. Jesus also spoke of the Holy Spirit as "the Spirit of Truth". Therefore if God is moving today in fulfilment of Joel's prophecy that he would pour out his Spirit upon all people, we may expect to see a movement of the Holy Spirit that will be a movement initiated by, led by and directed by the Spirit of Truth.

So what is there to worry about?

There is overwhelming evidence to support the belief that there is a new move of God today. A century ago there was a great move towards world evangelisation through the Nineteenth Century Missionary Movement. Today the move of God is not in sending out his servants to the ends of the earth, but in pouring out his Spirit upon believers everywhere. His intention is that they become evangelists within their own towns and villages, and that they become a Spirit-filled community through whom God is able to work in every location. Having sent the Gospel out in the last century God is now indigenising the Gospel, raising a people of power and the church is expanding and growing in maturity all over the world.

So what is there to worry about?

Surely, if God is in control, there is certainly nothing to worry about; as Paul says, "If God is for us, who can be against us?" He asks, "Who shall separate us from the love of Christ? Shall trouble or hardship or persecution, or famine or nakedness or danger or sword?" (Romans 8:31–35). He then declares his conviction that "neither death nor life, neither angels nor demons, neither the present nor the future, nor any powers, neither height nor depth, nor anything else in all creation, will be able to separate us from the love of God that is in Christ Jesus our Lord" (vv. 38–39). Paul is expressing his confidence in the ultimate victory of God over all opposition, both human and demonic, indeed over anything that could separate true believers from himself.

But Paul was also well aware of the battle situation facing us, hence his advice to the Ephesians to make sure they had the whole armour of God around them and to "stand firm then, with the belt of truth buckled round your waist" (Ephesians 6:14). What we are facing today, is not simply the opposition of men to the Gospel but the opposition of the principalities and powers of darkness. They introduce a whole new dimension to the battle of incredible subtlety that is often difficult to discern. The difference between spiritual truth and deception can only be discerned spiritually (1 Corinthians 2:14). The very nature of deception is that it is closely related to truth – otherwise it would deceive no one!

We have already noted how Moses discovered that the magicians "by their secret arts" were able to duplicate the miraculous powers he displayed. The enemy is able to counterfeit the miraculous. But there is a need to be alert to something infinitely more subtle than mere demonstrations of magical power. The Twentieth Century has seen the proliferation of cult and strange teachings and practice abounding among the sects and various sectors of the Church including mainline churches.

Signs of the Last Days?

Jesus gave specific warnings of what we may expect to see in the last days. If we are right in applying the prophecy of Joel to today, even though, as we have already stated, it began to be fulfilled nearly two thousand years ago in the apostolic age, then we must also take note of what is said in scripture concerning the last days. Jesus' words in Matthew 24 do not refer to Pentecost but to what may be the climax or closing period of "the last days"; in other words – the last days of the last days!

It is worth noting that Matthew records this discourse as being in response to questions put to Jesus by the disciples concerning his coming again and the end of the age. The "end of the age" is not the end of the world. An "age", in biblical usage, is simply a period of time of any duration that marks a stage in the fulfilment of the purposes of God.

It is also worth noting that before Jesus listed the "signs" he gave a solemn warning about deception "Watch out that no one deceives you". He then went on to list false christs, wars and revolutions, famines, earthquakes, (Luke adds strange diseases), persecution of believers, a falling away from the faith, false prophets, an increase in wickedness, the love of many believers growing cold. But Jesus also said "this Gospel of the Kingdom will be preached in the whole world as a testimony to all nations" (Matthew 24:3–14).

This is not the place to discuss the relevance of things Jesus foretold to events in our own day, although clearly many of what Jesus referred to as "signs of the end of the age" appear as news items in our daily newspapers and scenes on the TV news media. Our emphasis here is to pick out the warnings concerning deception, particularly the references to false Christs and false prophets.

What we are seeing today is a renewed onslaught of the principalities and powers of darkness designed to distort the truth and deceive the whole world, including the church. The church is, in fact, a special target of the enemy because she has been entrusted with God's truth. The attack is multi-directional, coming both from outside the church and from within. The external attack is more obvious and is often a frontal attack of the forces of secular humanism. The attack from within is more difficult to recognise (and to combat) as it usually takes some form of distorting the truth.

It is not only in the liberal churches, with their emphasis upon head knowledge, and their neglect of experience, where truth is distorted. Even among Bible-believing Christians, truth can be perverted by wrongly handling the word of God or by allowing the desires of the flesh and the values of the world to influence our teaching.

A good illustration of the way sound biblical truth can be perverted may be seen in what began as the "faith movement" where the emphasis is upon taking God at his word; standing on his promises; believing that God is encouraging us to ask and receive; we do not have, because we do not ask. This teaching was firmly grounded in scripture but it has led to some of the excesses of "prosperity teaching" and to what have been dubbed "name it and claim it" and "God wants you rich" cults where the emphasis has been less upon the necessity for faith and more on the material rewards.

A further example is the "shepherding movement" which emphasised the basic biblical concept of the shepherd caring for the sheep. Jesus referred to himself as the Good Shepherd who gave his life for the sheep and he charged the apostles with the task of tending the sheep and seeing that they were properly fed. David spoke of the Lord being his shepherd and leading him to green pastures as well as protecting him. But shepherding was never intended to become a cloak for authoritarianism and for exercising control over the lives of others as has happened in some of the strands of the House Church Movement.

This shepherding aberration may have come about as a result of a failure to understand the differences between the role of the shepherd in Middle Eastern culture and western practices. In Israel today, the shepherd goes ahead of his flock in the same way as he did in Jesus' day. The shepherd remains with his flock in the open countryside looking out for the best grass for them to feed upon and watching out at all times for the first sign of danger in order to protect them. This contrasts sharply with Western practices where the shepherd goes behind the flock, keeping the sheep in front of him and usually using a dog to snap at the sheep driving them in the direction of his choice. The sheep are simply driven, they do not follow. They have no choice in the matter. This has often been the characteristic of some strands of the charismatic church.

More recently shepherding or "heavy shepherding" has been widely criticised and many churches have been at pains to distance themselves from it, but certain elements of the spirit underlying the shepherding movement persist in many fellowships. The term "shepherding" has been dropped or changed to "covering" and more recently has become "accountability". It is of course, unarguable that we should all be accountable for our actions, and those exercising ministry should be accountable within the body of Christ, but we should never lose sight of the fact that it is Jesus who is the head of his Church and ultimately we are each of us directly and solely accountable to him. He is the true Shepherd of the sheep and he has never delegated this divine role to any human being however holy or spiritually gifted that person may be.

It is perhaps also worth remembering that the hired

shepherds in Jesus' day were never highly regarded for their faithfulness or for their commitment! They did not love the sheep in the same way as the owner of the sheep did. The owner of the sheep would lay down his life for the sheep. This is why Jesus stressed that he was the "Good Shepherd" and he constantly warned against the counterfeit – the false christs who would come among the flock to devour them like wolves. We are already seeing this today as part of the impact of the New Age movement.

From about 1975 New Agers began speaking publicly about "the christ" who was coming to lead the world into a new era of peace and prosperity. In 1979 there appeared a full page advertisement in a number of leading newspapers in major cities around the world announcing "THE CHRIST IS NOW HERE". The announcement said "We will recognise him by his extraordinary spiritual potency, the universality of his viewpoint and his love for all humanity. He comes not to judge, but to aid and inspire". It referred to the Christ as "Lord Maitreya, known by Christians as the Christ. And as Christians await the Second Coming, so the Jews await the Messiah, the Buddhists the fifth Buddha, the Muslims the Imam Mahdi, and the Hindus await Krishna. These are all names for one individual. *His presence in the world guarantees there will be no third world war*." The announcement went on to say "The Christ will acknowledge his identity and *within the next two months* will speak to humanity through a worldwide television and radio broadcast. His message will be heard inwardly, telepathically, by all people in their own language. From that time, with his help, we will build a new world."

In 1985, Benjamin Creme, the self-styled disciple of "the christ", announced that the Maitreya was living in East London, and explained that although he was "ready to emerge into public leadership and activity" he had not done so as previously announced because there had not been sufficient interest shown by the world's media. He was now awaiting the right time for his "reappearance", but in the meantime his message was being announced to the world through Creme. Creme leads meetings around the world giving messages which he claims to receive telepathically from the Maitreya. Basically the teaching is that men and women must learn to regard each other as brothers and sisters and must learn to share with each other. "This is a Truth, simple, but until now difficult for man to grasp. The time has come to evidence this Truth. By My Presence the Law of Sharing will become manifest. By My Presence man will grow to God . . ."

The Maitreya being promoted by Benjamin Creme is not the only false christ to be presented to the world today. There are numerous other teachers of esoteric religious systems, eastern gurus and leaders of cults who claim divinity or whose followers regard them as divine. Even the Afro-Caribbean cult of Ras Tafarianism is based upon a recognition of the late Haile Selassie, former Emperor of Ethiopia, as the christ.

False prophets are even more numerous than false christs. There have been an increasing number of them in recent years, some of whom have had disastrous effects upon the lives of their followers. They particularly aim to draw young people into their membership, and many of the cults use "thought reform" or brainwashing techniques to ensure that new recruits imbibe the teaching and will remain absolutely loyal to the group. One of the most dangerous aspects of the current cult phenomenon, which has accelerated since the 1960s, is their use of the Bible. Many of them take selected scriptures and base their doctrine upon them and they capitalise on their victim's ignorance of the whole witness of scripture.

Need for Doctrinal Truth

The only safeguard against the influence of the cults and the false teaching of those who promote false christs is to teach the truth. There is a wholeness of scripture that guarantees a grasp on the truth. Without this wholeness there can be an over-emphasis upon one aspect of the truth that leads to error. It is knowing the truth that sets us free, but the truth comes from the *whole* word of God and there is only One who was able to teach this wholeness because he had come from the Father and had been with the Father since the beginning of creation.

Jesus himself laid great emphasis upon knowing the truth. He used the phrase "I tell you the truth" time and time again throughout his life. The phrase is quoted seventy-nine times in the four Gospels. Additionally Jesus spoke many times about the truth in his disputes with the Pharisees and teachers of the law. He referred to the devil as a liar "when he lies, he speaks his native language, for he is a liar and the father of lies." Jesus went on to declare that he himself was telling the truth and "the reason you do not hear, is because you do not belong to God" (John 8:44–47). Jesus taught that anyone who belonged to the Father would be able to perceive the truth because the Holy Spirit, the Spirit of truth, would be in him. Without that Spirit of truth, he would be open to the deception of the father of lies.

Jesus was careful always to emphasise that it is the Father who is the ultimate source of truth, and his own mission was to accomplish the will of the Father who was working through him. "The words I say to you are not just my own. Rather, it is the Father, living in me, who is doing his work" (John 14:10). Jesus, nevertheless, declared that he and the Father were one, and because of this union with the Father, those who wished to know the truth should seek him. "I am the way and the truth and the life" he said (John

14:6). It is only as we declare the truth as it is revealed in Jesus through the power of the Holy Spirit, the Spirit of truth, that we are able to combat and to stand against the lies and deception of the false christs, false prophets and false teachers who are characteristic of the last days.

One of the greatest dangers facing the charismatic movement today is that doctrine has become unfashionable. At other times in history, when there has been a fresh move of God, such as in the Reformation and the Wesleyan Revival, theological debate featured prominently. The Reformation was a time of great learning, when both intellectuals and the ordinary people would travel long distances to listen to the great scholars and would be able to understand and participate in the subjects being discussed with considerable fervour. The Wesleyan Revival embraced ordinary working people and was founded upon small group meetings where everybody participated in the discussion of doctrine. Today the heavy emphasis is upon experience. Everyone has something to share but the things shared are spiritual experiences rather than differing points of doctrine.

If we lose sight of the importance of sound doctrine we become open to all kinds of error. God's enemy, who hates the truth, is quick to take advantage of this kind of situation. Responsible leaders should encourage every believer to study the Bible for themselves so that they know the truth. It is not enough to know what others have said about various passages of scripture, we each need to know the truth for ourselves. This is the only sure safeguard against the deception with which we are surrounded today.

Unfortunately, doctrine is a bore to the majority of believers today despite the obsession with listening to teaching tapes and attending conferences and Bible Weeks. The trend is one of unquestioning acceptance of everything given by the big-name speakers. The most popular meetings at these events are not the workshops, where truths can be worked out and applied, or even the seminars where questions can be asked, but the celebrations where everyone can participate in the times of worship and enjoy the entertaining discourses of popular speakers. The most acceptable speakers are not those who give deep theological truths but those who recount experiential anecdotes and who promise great things to all believers.

This emphasis on the experiential is largely a reaction away from the over-emphasis upon head knowledge in the traditional churches. This led to an intellectualisation of the faith that often left the ordinary church members behind. The great preachers, who occupied the pulpits and filled the pews of large churches in the Nineteenth Century and early Twentieth Century, gave way to the sterile biblical criticism that characterised the liberal churches, while evangelical doctrine tended to become more and more the domain of the professional theologian, all of which tended to alienate the ordinary believer from the realm of doctrine. Probably the one exception to this was the Brethren, who in any case did not have professional clergy.

The charismatic movement, like all new movements, has tended to reflect things that were missing in the traditional churches. A major emphasis has been upon "participation" in reaction to the stifling effects of the traditional clergy-led churches. The newer churches began as small group meetings or house churches and threw up their own leaders, most of whom had little or no formal theological training. Many of these are now in senior positions of leadership and while it would not be true to say that they despise doctrine, the tendency is to concentrate on their own teachings rather than allow their people to be open to the wider theological debates. Doctrinal debate, therefore, tends to be incestuous and lacks the healthy critical forum of comparison with teaching and biblical interpretation that emanates from other parts of the body of Christ. There is grave danger in this because it results in the uncritical acceptance of error from ideas that have been passed around and have become accepted through constant repetition, but which were originally based upon *experience* rather than sound biblical interpretation and have never been subjected to searching academic scrutiny.

It is interesting to note how the same old heresies such as Gnosticism and Arianism recur time after time in different forms. Those who are not familiar with early church history or who have never made a detailed academic study of early church dogma are not so alert to these recurring problems throughout the history of the Church.

A good example is to be seen in the way the teachings of the "Latter Rain" movement recur in so many of the current strands of the charismatic churches. Although John Wimber and Mike Bickle, representing Anaheim/KCF leadership, stated in July 1990 that they did not accept Latter Rain teaching, the fact is that the ideas and teachings that have been coming out of the KCF-led "prophetic movement" since 1983 have borne striking resemblance to the teachings of the Latter Rain movement.

Franklin Hall is usually regarded as the father of the movement which began in 1946 with the establishment of a "fasting and prayer daily revival centre" in San Diego. In that year, Franklin Hall published a book *Atomic Power with God through Fasting and Prayer* (Phoenix: Hall Deliverance Foundation) that had a significant impact on the whole Pentecostal world. Hall advocated long periods of fasting and went so far as to state "without fasting, prayer becomes ineffectual" (p.9). Hall regarded fasting as so essential that it would be effective regardless of the God to whom prayer was made. He said, "Many, if not all, the American Indian tribes sought revelation of the Great Spirit through Prayer and Fasting. When they had famines, food shortages, lack of rain, etc, the Great Spirit was sought through prayer and fasting, and their prayers were answered" (p.19).

One of the outstanding elements in Hall's teaching was his belief that Christians can actually become immortal through progressive stages of spiritual growth. His teachings on attaining immortality in this life through psycho-spiritual exercises and through "holiness" or righteous living, have provided the foundation upon which many subsequent teachings in the charismatic/restoration churches have been based. Hall believed that in the last days a generation would arise who will experience "real gushers and torrents of the long, past due, RAIN OF RIGHTEOUSNESS. A rain of IMMORTALITY UPON THE EARTH that so many prophets have written about and portrayed in their prophecies ... permanent, lasting freedoms from all sickness, harmful, accident things and defeat will come about. Freedom from the imprisonment of all gravitational forces will also be brought upon the whole man. This study teaches one the power and secrets of space flight, space flotation and hovering ability. It gives the Bible formula for weightlessness, the 'raising up' power of those who come to immortality (John 6 and Romans 2:7)" (Franklin Hall, *The Return of Immortality*, Phoenix: Hall Deliverance Foundation, Inc, 1976 pp.2–3).

It is not always recognised that there were strong occult elements in Hall's teaching. He spoke of UFOs (Unidentified Flying Objects) and UHOs (Unusual Heavenly Objects) and IHOs (Immortal Heavenly Objects). "The sparkling shining fine gold and silver are seen upon their skin, brought about through the faith-power of impartation. The polished brass, the beryl stone appearances are even now manifested today." Hall promised that those attending his meetings (*International Holy Ghost and Fire Seminars*) would receive "the shiny metal-like Jesus substance" on their bodies (ibid p.20).

At the age of eighty, Hall was still giving this teaching when he spoke to a meeting in 1988. He said that he did not have the authority to grant full immortality but believers could receive immortality "up to their knees". He invited people to come to the front to receive this "special Holy Ghost anointing".

The teaching given by the Kansas City Prophets on the subject of the special power that is going to be exercised by the last generation preceding the Second Coming of Christ, bears remarkable similarity to Hall's teaching. They believe the generation born since 1973 to be the "special generation" marked out by God for this anointing and therefore the present generation of believers have a particular responsibility for training them, although they themselves will have limited immortality.

They refer to the children as "an elected seed generation and an endtime/Omega generation who will possess the Spirit without measure as the manifested sons of God". They will do "ten thousand times the miracles in the Book of Acts. They will move their hands and the power of God will go like flashes of lightning, and as they go like this over a million people, if a person is missing an arm, it will instantly be created . . . they will walk through walls . . . they will be translated . . . hundreds of dead will be raised during meetings in ball park stadiums." They will speak to meetings of a million or more people when multitudes will be saved; amazing miracles will take place such as "eyes put back in eye sockets"; they will be invincible and immortal; they will be used to confound unbelievers and subdue the nations (from KCF tapes).

It is difficult to know exactly what KCF currently believe since their June 1990 statement acknowledging fifteen areas of error, the thirteenth of which was "using jargon that reflects the teaching of groups that we do not wish to be identified with". This was linked with a statement denying any association with the Latter Rain movement but it would appear that it is not the doctrine itself which they are wishing to distance themselves from, but only the use of jargon reflecting the teaching of these groups. The publicity for the October 1990 meetings in Britain contained the statement "God is raising up a new breed of 'dread warriors', and the speakers will issue apostolic, prophetic, evangelistic and pastoral calls to join the new breed." This reference to "a new breed of dread warriors" looks remarkably like the teaching KCF have been giving for a number of years, which in turn looks remarkably like the teaching of Franklin Hall.

They repented of "teaching or implying that KCF and Vineyard are an elite group or that we are the leaders of a new elite group about to be revealed by God" (point 12), and they also repented of "manifesting an attitude of superiority through the possession of a secret body of information" (point 15) but they did not specify any particular doctrine that they had come to recognise as error.

They made a vague reference to false doctrine in that they repented of "the attempt by some prophetic ministers to establish doctrine or practice by revelation alone, apart from clear biblical support" (point 2). But they did not say which doctrines they were abandoning. The printed teaching notes issued to conference participants at Holy Trinity, Brompton, London in July 1990 referred to some prophets receiving a "constant flow of revelationary information" and being "more at home in heaven than on earth" and others who "will receive words, dreams, visions daily, or at least very regularly. Will have 'open visions' at least occasionally (i.e. angelic visitations, theophanies, audible voice)." All of which sounds very much like the teaching KCF have been giving for a number of years that "the end time/Omega generation super-church will do ten thousand times the miracles in the Book of Acts". This is a statement for which there is no biblical support, but it probably comes out of Bob Jones' personal claims to having "between five and ten visions every night" and since 1974 to "seeing angels ten to fifteen times a week" (KCF tapes of Mike Bickle interviewing Bob Jones).

Although the KCF leadership say they have repented of establishing doctrine or practice by revelation alone, it is not at all clear whether they are aware of the extent to which their teaching has been based upon revelationary experience. After having listened to many hours of KCF tapes and studying many of their written statements, it would appear that the prophets encourage one another by confirming each other's prophecies and picking up each other's visions and adding to them. As each one is built upon, it becomes more fantastic with wild prophecies of imminent revival and promises of supernatural power and amazing exploits to be performed by believers who join the movement. It is these promises that are attracting many immature believers to their meetings and to respond to their calls to join the "new breed" and to participate in the promised exploits. These promises have no basis in scripture and reflect more of the desires of the flesh than the true biblical word of God.

The great danger is that this teaching will prove to be a massive hindrance to the true prophetic movement which is a genuine work of the Holy Spirit throughout the world today. God is undoubtedly calling people to new standards of personal holiness and commitment and it is perfectly true that God is speaking to his people prophetically today, but where wild promises of supernatural power are made, promising the people all the fleshly things that they would love to receive, this will inevitably be followed by great disappointment. The resulting disillusionment with prophecy which has proved false will have the serious effect of undermining the credibility of genuine prophecy in the minds of believers.

True prophecy always has a radical cutting edge that is in vivid contrast to the standards of the world. The true prophetic word of God rarely leaves the hearers feeling comfortable. It certainly *does* bring comfort to true believers, through the knowledge that the Lord is with them and speaking to them, but it is never a *comfortable* word promising easy costless blessings. The truly prophetic word of God will always challenge the Church as well as the world.

Jeremiah continually faced problems with the false prophets who told the people the very kind of things that they wanted to hear. He pleaded with the people not to pay any heed to them "Do not listen to what the prophets are prophesying to you; they fill you with false hopes. They speak visions out of their own minds, not from the mouth of the Lord" (Jeremiah 23:16).

We would like to emphasise that we are not despising experiential knowledge but we are emphasising the need for it to be accepted only in conjunction with a careful study of scripture. Certainly we do not wish to see the church return to a heavy emphasis upon head knowledge which could well be the result of a reaction against error coming in from an over-emphasis upon the experiential.

As a Pharisee, Paul had to face this problem. In his letter to the Philippians he speaks with pride of his Hebrew background and his training in the law. He nevertheless goes on to say "but whatever was to my profit I now consider loss for the sake of Christ" (3:4–7). Paul never forgot the experience on the road to Damascus that brought about a total change in his life. His encounter with Christ was entirely experiential. In fact, Paul boasted to the Galatians that he received the whole of the Gospel that he preached "by revelation from Jesus Christ" (Galatians 1:12).

This experience must have contrasted sharply with Paul's academic background. His testimony in Jerusalem was that he had been educated "in this city. Under Gamaliel I was thoroughly trained in the law of our fathers" (Acts 22:3). It could not have been easy for Paul to make the adjustment from his legalistic academic way of thinking to the sudden intrusion of a revelationary experience into his life. It was probably for this reason that he left Damascus and according to his own testimony "went immediately into Arabia" (Galatians 1:17). No doubt, when he was alone with the Lord in Arabia, Paul would have meditated on such scriptures as Isaiah 29:14 that he quoted when writing to the Corinthians "I will destroy the wisdom of the wise; the intelligence of the intelligent I will frustrate." Paul went on to say to the Corinthians that God chooses the foolish things, the weak things and the lowly things of this world "so that no one may boast before him" (1 Corinthians 1:29).

Paul had realised that none of his great learning was able to bring him into that right relationship with God for which in his great zeal for the law he had always longed. He was forced by his own experience to the conclusion that it is only through God's gracious love in revealing his truth to us that we are able to be saved.

Paul, nevertheless, did not abandon his intellectual capacity. He used it to give a carefully reasoned account of his faith on many occasions such as when he was invited to address the Athenian philosophers in the meeting of the Areopagus (Acts 17:22f). It is also perfectly clear to anyone who has attempted to study the deep theological truths expressed in the letter to the Romans that Paul had by no means abandoned his powers of intellectual reasoning.

In Paul we find a perfect blend of spiritual revelation and intellect. He believed that all spiritual truth is spiritually discerned; he went so far as to say that he preached the Gospel "not in words taught us by human wisdom, but in words taught by the Spirit, expressing spiritual truths in spiritual words" (1 Corinthians 2:13). But he, nevertheless, urged the Corinthians to use their minds in a proper way. He exhorted them "Brothers, stop thinking like children. In regard to evil be infants, but in your thinking be adults" (1 Corinthians 14:20). In matters of personal morality, Paul wanted the believers to be as innocent as little children, but in matters concerning doctrine, he wanted them to exercise the intellect of *adults* and the maturity of age so that they would not be deceived by false teachers and false prophets who would come among them.

Discernment and Deception

Paul warned the Colossians "see to it that no one takes you captive through hollow and deceptive philosophy, which depends on human tradition and the basic principles of this world rather than on Christ" (Colossians 2:8). He instructed the Thessalonians that in their handling of prophetic revelation they must "test everything. Hold on to the good. Avoid every kind of evil" (1 Thessalonians 5:21–22).

This is advice that the Church urgently needs to heed today. We constantly need to bear in mind Jesus' warning that the last days would be days of deception when many deceivers would be active, even among believers. Even men who love the Lord, and know that God is indeed speaking to his people today with prophetic revelationary knowledge, may mislead the people. They can do this through failing to recognise, or to teach adequately, the *reason why* God is speaking prophetically today. The new prophetic movement has to be seen against the background of *contemporary world events in the context of biblical prophetic revelation.*

When the activity of God today, in pouring out his Spirit upon all believers, is not presented clearly within this biblical framework, there are grave dangers. These dangers become acute if the teaching is linked to signs and wonders and promises of supernatural power but is not rooted in a right understanding of the *fulfilment of the purposes of God* as revealed in scripture. It is only as we see God working out his purposes today that our eyes are turned towards him and away from ourselves. This ensures that all the glory is given to God and guards us against indulging in the self-gratifying nature of the flesh, or being deceived by the appealing nature of any teaching which may be easy on the ears and coated with spiritual sweetness.

In February 1990, thousands attended meetings at Anaheim, California to hear prophetic messages given in a *Holiness Unto The Lord* conference. During one of these meetings, Paul Cain was telling the people about the great power that was coming to them in the revival that would soon be sweeping across the nation. They would be participants in this and he promised them that they did not have to go out of the hall that night without receiving some of this power. In a period of eloquent oratory, he worked upon the emotions of the crowd giving them word pictures of the mighty deeds they would perform and the immense power they would possess. This would enable them to perform supernatural deeds which would not only restore sight to the blind and make the lame walk but also confound unbelievers and eventually subdue the nations.

At the climax of this speech, the whole conference were on their feet shouting and cheering and clapping and applauding; but to anyone listening soberly to the tape, unaffected by the emotion of the conference hall, the questionableness of the message is self-evident. Indeed in listening to hundreds of tapes that have come out of the various strands of the new prophetic movement that is currently exciting many people in America, there is a notable absence of reference to the basic elements of the Gospel.

Those elements missing include the Cross; sin and redemption; the necessity for new birth; even references to the Holy Spirit are rare. There is plenty of talk about "the spirit" or "a new wave of the spirit", but rarely reference to the work of *the Holy Spirit* in biblical context. The great danger of this lack of Bible-centred teaching is that is panders to the desires of the people and raises false hopes of supernatural power not simply being given at some vague future point in history, but actually becoming the possession of people now. It ignores the fact that all the spiritual gifts are the gift of God. Prophets are not created by the laying on of hands. You cannot *teach* people to be prophets. They can only receive ministry gifts if the call of God is upon their lives. No one can become a prophet by the enthusiastic response to calls to join a new movement and become part of a new army of "dread warriors" or some special "new breed" of mankind possessing superior powers.

"Kingdom Now" or "Dominion" teaching is being developed in many groups in the USA by leaders such as Earl Paulk. In *Harvestime* (his church newsletter), October 1984, he declared, "Atlanta, Watch out! Ready or not, here comes a local church convinced that it is God's time for us to take the kingdom and restore it to the government of God. We are convinced that divine principles in this church are incompatible with the world, so we are going to change the world. The church is God's enforcement agency for implementing divine government here and now."

Paulk describes as "false prophets" any who oppose his teaching. He says "If a prophet comes who attempts to lead us away from truths established by revelation, he is a false prophet. But we do not need to worry about dealing with him because God already has a plan for taking care of him. 'That prophet shall be put to death'." The grave danger here is that Paulk is teaching that truths can be "established by *revelation*" whereas truth has already been established by scripture and it is only heresies that seek to add to scripture. Paul referred the Corinthians to the saying "Do not go beyond what is written" (1 Corinthians 4:6) and Peter spoke of the word of God standing for ever (1 Peter 1:25).

Peter made special reference to prophecy that was established in scripture having been given by God himself "No prophecy of scripture came about by the prophet's own interpretation. For prophecy never had its origin in the will of man, but men spoke from God as they were carried along by the Holy Spirit" (2 Peter 1:20–21). But Peter also warned that "there will be false teachers among you. They will secretly introduce destructive heresies . . . many will follow their shameful ways and will bring the way of truth into disrepute. In their greed these teachers will exploit you with stories they have made up" (2 Peter 2:1–3).

The aggressive teaching of Paulk is carried even farther by Al Jandl, pastor of the Living Stones. In his book *The Mandate*, he writes, "Church, God is saying 'I have given you authority, whatever you won't allow, I won't allow. Whatever you do allow, I will allow' . . . All of a sudden in my spirit, these words came up and before I thought about them I said out loud, 'I don't care what God allows, I don't allow it' . . . I have a mandate from God, authority to rule over a defeated territory. What I allow on earth (loose) God will allow. What I don't allow (bind) God won't allow. The control of our country, the offices of our government isn't just a haphazard up-in-the-air deal. The control of what happens isn't just up to God . . . God has put the control of the earth in our hands." Jandl appears to have usurped the sovereignty of God and actually taken upon himself divine authority. The Bible declares that "the government is upon his shoulders", referring to Messiah – the Lord Jesus Christ – not upon ours.

The false prophets are active in the Church today, even among believers, like wolves running loose among the sheep. They tell the people the things they want to hear. They promise good tidings of great joy. "Peace! Peace!", they cry, and the people love it. They promise them they will possess divine power, power to convince unbelievers, power to subdue the nations and the people flock to hear the message. Teaching of this sort is simply spiritual seduction, playing upon the desire of the fleshly nature to exercise power and hence to gain recognition also.

These promises of supernatural power come from the same spirit as the New Age teaching that promises the people they can become gods. The New Age movement represents a far greater threat to the Church than most people realise. It is not only the liberal intellectuals who are open to New Age influence, but all those who are not thoroughly grounded in the truth and constantly seeking the Lord in humility. Wherever the values of the world, or the desires of the flesh, have penetrated Christian defences, New Age teaching will make a strong appeal.

The subtlety of New Age teaching lies in the fact that it makes truth its starting point. It speaks of love, freedom, peace, harmony – all of which are to be found in the Bible. But New Age theology actually reverses the Gospel. The Gospel declares that God became man. New Age theology says that man can become God. This concept of man becoming God is central to the new theology of "Creation-Centred Spirituality" devised by Father Matthew Fox, the Dominican theologian and scholar who in 1977 founded the Institute in Culture and Creation Spirituality in California. The essence of Fox's teaching is an attempt to overcome the dualism inherent in Christianity between spirit and matter and the "hegemony of fall/redemption theology" (*Original Blessing*, Bear & Co 1983 p.l80). His objective is to overcome the guilt implanted into man by what he sees as the false teaching of traditional Judaeo/Christian beliefs in the fall and original sin. His objective is to enable mankind to re-enter the original state of blessing which existed in a harmony with nature.

In doing so Fox says "We become like the Creator and take on the Creator's characteristics" (*Whee! We, Wee All the Way Home*, Bear & Co 1981 p 79). He teaches that just as God indwells the whole of creation, so when man immerses himself in creation, he thereby becomes God. He speaks of "our growth into divinity" (*Original Blessing*, p.85). We can enter this mystical union with the world of natural creation by a variety of means such as fasting, chanting, yoga, zen, transcendental meditation and even through drug taking. He sees all of these as acceptable means of "attaining the experience of God" and overcoming the duality of man/God and man/nature and thereby entering into our true spiritual state of harmony with nature through which we become God.

Creation-Centred Spirituality is becoming accepted as the major theological expression of the New Age movement. Fox is not worried by charges that his teaching is not scriptural because he sees the Bible as a collection of "man-made word books" (ibid, p.38). Creation-Centred Spirituality Centres are springing up all over Britain as well as in other parts of the world, notably the USA. In America the major centre is in the Cathedral of St John the Divine, New York, whereas in Britain it is in St James's, Piccadilly, an Anglican church in the fashionable West End of London. Most of these centres in Britain are led by ordained clergy but it is not only the Church of England that has been infiltrated by New Age teaching, ministers of many denominations are involved.

Creation-Centred Spirituality is rapidly taking its place as the theology of the New Age movement and has strong links with both the ecumenical and the inter-faith movements. In a leaflet published by St James's Church, Piccadilly, advertising meetings to be addressed by Matthew Fox in July 1990, it said that "Creation-Centred Spirituality is rooted in the wisdom and insights of the mystical tradition contained in all major religions". On 20th April 1989, St James's, Piccadilly celebrated Wesak – the Birthday of the Buddha – at what they called "an interdenominational meditation ceremony in the church"; saying that "for many people in the New Age Movement this is the most important spiritual event of the year".

The extent to which the inter-faith movement has penetrated the Church of England may be gauged from the fact that on 12th March 1990, the Queen in company with many leaders in the nation, attended the annual observance for Commonwealth Day held in Westminster Abbey. The service included a reading from the *Suta-Nipata*, a Buddhist holy book, read by the Acting High Commissioner for Sri Lanka; a reading from the *Sveta-vatara Upanishad*, a Hindu text urging the worship of Brahman; a reading from the *Qur'an*, the Islamic holy book, read by the High Commissioner for Pakistan. A Buddhist monk chanted, in Pali, praise to the Buddha; a Hindu Swami chanted, in Sanskrit, a prayer on the theme of seeking Nirvana; a Muslim Imam chanted, in Arabic, praise to Allah; and a Sikh leader chanted, in Punjabi, praise to the god who is the true guru who "is everywhere and in everyone". All the religious leaders prayed to their own gods and chanted their prayers in their own languages, but there was no mention of the Lord Jesus throughout the service, not even in the hymns or the Bible reading. Yet Westminster Abbey was the place where Queen Elizabeth the Second was crowned in 1953 and took her solemn oaths to defend and uphold the biblical Protestant Reformed tradition of the Christian Church.

The St James's leaflet on Creation-Centred Spirituality noted its links with others who share the "creation-centred perspective". Among those listed were the Iona Community, the World Council of Churches and various interfaith projects. It also listed ICOREC (International Consultancy on Religion, Education and Culture) and the World Wildlife Fund. It is these two bodies that have been most active in promoting ecology-awareness events in British cathedrals.

WWF have sponsored a number of cathedral-based Creation Festivals following their twenty-fifth anniversary inter-faith celebration at Assisi in 1986. The first in Britain was a Harvest Thanksgiving held in Winchester Cathedral in 1987. During this service, what has become known as the "Rainbow Covenant" devised by Martin Palmer, Director of ICOREC, was introduced. In *Lord of Creation* (p.38), Palmer traces the Hindu origins of this practice known as "Raksha Bandha" in which sisters tie rainbow threads around the wrists of brothers in order to pass on to them earth's creative energies. The entire congregation in Winchester tied rainbow threads around the wrists of their neighbours, symbolising the establishing of a three-way covenant between God, humankind and nature. According to the WWF, the ceremony has since been used in thousands of churches and schools throughout the UK. It is said to be a popular feature of multi-faith acts of worship.

It is this multi-faith element in worship that concerns many evangelical Christians because they fear that it can lead to inter-faith activities that undermine the uniqueness of the Gospel. Inter-faith activities form part of the programme of the New Age Movement whose ultimate objective is to establish a New World Order. This New World Order consists of three parts – a world economy, a world government, and a world religion. The global economic system will be managed by a centralised world government supported by a single united one-world religion.

New Agers have realised that it is not possible to achieve their objectives in a single leap; clearly the failure of the League of Nations and the United Nations to establish world government demonstrates this. The plan now being followed is known as "piecemeal functionalism" through which the most powerful globalist groups work through a variety of institutions, crossing national boundaries to accomplish specific tasks piece by piece until the time is right when the pieces can be fitted together like a giant jigsaw puzzle.

Part of the technique of achieving their aims by this strategy is through "crisis management" whereby crises – economic, political or environmental – are either created or, if they occur naturally, exploited through widespread publicity. When sufficient alarm has been created global solutions to the crisis are proposed. These solutions are accepted under crisis pressures when they would never have been given consideration under normal circumstances. Many examples of the piecemeal approach can be seen today in the pollution crisis, the ozone layer depletion, deforestation, the population crisis, the arms race crisis, the third world debt crisis, the Gulf oil crisis, the Middle East/Palestinian/ Lebanon/hostages crisis. All these issues heightened by the world media will eventually coalesce through the threat to world peace and global destruction to force the whole of mankind to accept global solutions to what will eventually be presented as one gigantic global crisis.

This is not the place to consider the eschatological significance of the New Age movement in terms of the fulfilment of biblical prophecy but it is worth noting in passing that these three strands of the New World Order are all envisaged in the Revelation of St John in reference to the reign of the antichrist.

World Government is seen in Revelation 13:7 "He was given power to make war against the saints and to conquer them. And he was given authority over every tribe, people, language and nation."

World Economy is seen in Revelation 13: 16–17 "He also forced everyone, small and great, rich and poor, free and slave, to receive a mark on his right hand or on his forehead, so that no one could buy or sell unless he had the mark."

World Religion is seen in Revelation 13:4, "Men worshipped the dragon because he had given authority to the beast, and they also worshipped the beast."

A single religious system plays an essential part in legitimizing the new world order and it is for this reason that New Agers are paying such attention to the development of inter-faith and ecumenical links and are using the deeply-held concerns of people in the different religions for world peace and for environmental issues.

Dr Robert Muller, Chancellor of the New Age "University for Peace" and former Assistant Secretary General for Economic and Social Development at the United Nations, said at a conference in Costa Rica in June 1989 "I hope that religious leaders will get together and define . . . what God, or the gods, or the cosmos are expecting from humans . . . We must hope also that the Pope will come before the year 2000 to the United Nations, speak for all the religions and spiritualities on this planet and give the world the religious view of how the third millennium should be a spiritual millennium, a millennium which will see the integration and harmony of humanity with creation, with nature, with the planet, with the cosmos and with eternity" (*World Goodwill Newsletter*, 1989, no 4).

The grave dangers represented by the New Age movement and the false teachers, false messiahs and false prophets that have gone out into the world and are active today even among believers should be obvious, yet the subtleties of their teachings are by no means so obvious, and the persuasiveness with which the cults present their appeal to young people has been the cause of many personal tragedies in the past few decades. Any realistic assessment of the signs of the times in which we live must surely point to an increase in deception and an increasing onslaught upon those who stand firm in the revealed faith and in the centrality of the Christian belief that there is salvation in no other name than that of the Lord Jesus Christ. Jesus warned that even the elect would be in danger of deception during the last days of this age.

What exposes even believers to deception is lack of understanding of the truth. Perhaps the greatest need today is for a thorough knowledge of the whole of Scripture together with clear discernment. Discernment is a mark of spiritual maturity which comes through a right understanding of the word of God which is the solid food referred to in Hebrews: "Solid food is for the mature, who by constant use have trained themselves to distinguish good from evil" (5:14). Thus it is through familiarity with scripture, being soaked in the word of God, that we become so familiar with the truth that it becomes a part of us. When the truth is living within us, it is not difficult to discern the lies, counterfeit spirituality and deception of the enemy.

Those involved in high street banking recognise the necessity for counter staff to be able quickly to recognise counterfeit bank notes, and that this is best achieved by familiarity with every detail of genuine notes. They realise that it is more important to know the real thing than to study the forgeries. In this day of deception when the enemy is actively sowing tares among the wheat, our strongest defence lies in standing firm with the belt of truth buckled around our waist, to use Paul's metaphor of the whole armour of God in Ephesians 6:10f. The belt was an essential part of the Roman soldier's armour as it buckled together every part around his body. It held the whole armour firmly together. This is the function of the truth given to us in the word of God.

Paul warned Timothy that "the Spirit clearly says that in later times some will abandon the faith and follow deceiving spirits and things taught by demons" (1 Timothy 4:1). He also foresaw that the coming of the antichrist would be accompanied by a display of "all kinds of counterfeit miracles, signs and wonders" (2 Thessalonians 2:9). Paul went on to say that people perish because they do not love the truth (v.10). The advice given in Hebrews 5:14 for those who desire to attain spiritual maturity is that they must train themselves by constant practice to distinguish good from evil.

The three principal reasons given in the New Testament for people being duped by lies and deception are:

1. At the time of conversion, they make only a superficial response to the Gospel. This is the teaching of Jesus in the parable of the sower. He says that the seed sown among thorns is "the man who hears the word, but worries of this life and the deceitfulness of wealth choke it, making it unfruitful" (Matthew 13:22).

2. They refuse to accept the truth because it is unpleasant. "They say to the seers 'see no more visions!' and to the prophets, 'give us no more visions of what is right! Tell us pleasant things, prophesy illusions . . . Stop confronting us with the Holy One of Israel!'" (Isaiah 30:10–11).

3. They neglect to make use of the supernatural gift of discerning between spirits (1 Corinthians 12:10) which is available to all Spirit-filled believers. Paul says we should "eagerly desire spiritual gifts" (1 Corinthians 14:1) and Jesus reminds us that God who is our loving Father is longing to give us all good gifts if we will ask him with pure

hearts, seeking first the kingdom and his righteousness (Matthew 6:33).

The only final safeguard against deception is to be thoroughly familiar with the truth, to study the word of God as Paul advised Timothy to do in order to show himself a workman approved by God "who rightly handles the word of truth" (2 Timothy 2:15). This should be the objective of every believer as we move farther into the last days and deeper into the days of deception and nearer to the Second Coming of him who alone is the Truth.

Chapter Seven

The New Prophetic Movement

Undoubtedly we live in extraordinary times. We began this book by referring to the rapid and radical changes that have been occurring in the world and gaining increasing momentum throughout the Twentieth Century. Advances in technology and communications have resulted in local or regional issues becoming global crises. Everyone familiar with biblical prophecy knows that the eschatological picture presented there is of global conflict focusing upon the Middle East.

Before these events take place God has promised a great outpouring of his Spirit to bring about a mighty spiritual harvest for the kingdom. This will take place at a time of great international upheaval when not only the nations are shaken (social, political and economic systems), but also the whole realm of natural creation.

It is not our purpose to give detailed evidence of this in contemporary events although it would not be difficult to do so. Our purpose is to note the rise of a new prophetic movement which we believe is a fulfilment of the promises of God and in particular of the prophecy of Joel 2:28–30. We have been noting much of the evidence for this together with the warning signs that Jesus gave concerning deception. It is our intention in this final chapter to summarise the evidence, particularly as we ourselves have noted it on our ministry travels around the world.

Signs of a New Prophetic Movement

We have noticed twelve significant signs of the fulfilment of biblical prophecy that together indicate the emergence of a new prophetic movement today.

1. Worldwide Growth of the Church

The first sign of the contemporary prophetic movement has to be the outstanding growth of the Church in the second half of the Twentieth Century. At least one third of the entire population of the world now acknowledge themselves to be Christians. Approximately 130 million new believers come to Christ every year, and at least sixty-five new churches are planted every day. The rate of growth of both believers and new fellowships is actually increasing, and in many areas of the world it is similar to the growth rate of the Church in the apostolic age and the first centuries of the Christian era. In some parts of the world, such as in central and southern Africa, the spiritual new-birth rate actually exceeds that of the natural birth rate.

The present rapid expansion of the Church is notable for bringing about a major demographic change. It is significant that the main growth has taken place in what we know as Third World countries which is having the effect of changing the focal point of the Christian world. Whereas at the beginning of the Twentieth Century the majority of Christians were in Europe and North America and a minority were in the rest of the world, today that position has been reversed. There has been a significant shift from the northern hemisphere to the southern hemisphere and from west to east.

The growth in the number of new believers in China is the most spectacular, and is outstripping that of any other nation in the world. There are vast numbers of new believers coming to faith throughout South–East Asia which until recently was considered the most difficult area for the Gospel in the world. The recent growth in all these nations has not come through western missions but through the outpouring of the Spirit of God upon nationals. It is the local people who have become the evangelists and who are bringing their unbelieving neighbours to Christ.

A large proportion of the current worldwide growth is in the Pentecostal/charismatic sector of the Church. The growth in this sector has not only been seen in the planting of new churches but has resulted in a new wave of spirituality in many older more traditional churches. What has come to be known as the "Third Wave" of the Holy Spirit to be poured out during this century has transformed many churches which would call themselves neither Pentecostal nor charismatic.

The spectacular growth of the Church in this century is a fulfilment of the promises and purposes of God spoken of in many prophecies in the Bible. We have already referred to a number of these such as Haggai 2:6–7 where the great spiritual harvest is linked with the shaking of the nations; Joel 2:28 and the outpouring of the Spirit of God upon all people; and Matthew 24:14 where Jesus said that the Gospel would be "preached in the whole world".

Jesus undoubtedly envisaged a time when his commission to the disciples to "go and make disciples of all nations" would be literally fulfilled. His instruction to teach them "to obey everything I have commanded you" was linked with the eschatological promise "And surely I am with you always, to the very end of the age" (Matthew

28:19–20). This implies that Jesus did not expect the Great Commission to be completely fulfilled until the end of the age. The vast scale of world evangelisation, taking the Gospel to all nations, could not be carried out by the Twelve, or even the 120 at Pentecost. It would require the mobilisation and motivation of believers in all the nations to reach all peoples everywhere. This could only be accomplished through a worldwide outpouring of the Holy Spirit.

2. The Lordship of Jesus

A second mark of the new prophetic movement is the recognition of the Lordship of Jesus by millions of his people today. People of all cultures are giving honour to the name of Jesus and acknowledging his headship over his Church. This is leading to greater trust and obedience and faithfulness among his people. The inevitable result of this increased faithfulness is seen in a purified Church, especially in those areas less subjected to the pressures of secular materialism such as constantly assail the Church in the West.

Throughout the world today there is a new sense of the presence of Jesus in his Church that is bringing fresh joy and hope even to those in situations of hardship, poverty or persecution. Jesus has become personally known to millions of believers in the East, in vivid contrast to the remoteness of the gods they formerly worshipped in Hinduism and Buddhism. A similar experience is taking place in the West in the lives of those who are discovering or rediscovering the presence of Jesus in a new way through charismatic renewal.

The name of Jesus is honoured today through praise and worship in a way probably not seen since the days of the Early Church, when the presence of Jesus was vividly real. This is a time when hundreds of new songs are being composed and sung in praise of Jesus, many of which are being translated into numerous languages. For those privileged to travel widely and to share in worship with believers in different parts of the world, there is a very real sense of belonging to one family and being able to participate in praise and worship even without knowing the language. When the name of Jesus is lifted up by his people, the barriers of race, nationality and culture disappear. The Lordship of Jesus is creating a new international spiritual unity that is setting the scene for the fulfilment of the prophecy that the day will come when "in the name of Jesus every knee shall bow".

A notable feature of worship today is that songs of praise are often addressed *to* Jesus rather than simply *about* him. Prayer also has become much more personal, with people praying *to Jesus* rather than simply *saying formal prayers*. This reflects the new emphasis not only upon the Lordship of Jesus in his Church but also upon the personal relationship of each believer with him.

This personal relationship with the Lord Jesus can be seen as a fulfilment of the prophecy of Jeremiah 31:31, where the effects of the New Covenant between God and his people were foreseen. This would lead to each believer knowing God for themselves and not having to rely upon the testimony of others. The personal experience of the Lordship of Jesus in our lives is one of the results of the outpouring of the Holy Spirit upon all believers. It brings a new dimension into the life of each individual believer, that transforms them from nominal adherents of a religious system to active participants in the mission of Christ.

3. Ordinary People Spirit-Filled

One of the outstanding marks of the new prophetic movement that is a clear fulfilment of the prophecy of Joel, is that the Spirit of God is being poured out upon ordinary people. It is not simply the rich and the powerful, neither is it the learned and those of high status, who are being filled with the Spirit. God is moving mightily among the people, the humble poor in many nations. They are the ones who are rejoicing in the Lordship of Jesus and who are experiencing the joy of being favoured by God. Their joy is similar to that which Mary expressed in the Magnificat, when she realised how God had favoured her and how he turned upside-down the expectations of the world. She foresaw the prophetic significance of God's action in the incarnation and that the day would come when the rich and the proud would be overthrown and the humble poor exalted.

The prophecy of Joel similarly foretold the effects of the Spirit of God being poured out upon all people. It would be received in full measure by those who were servants, because God is no respecter of persons. Today we are seeing the gifts of the Spirit in the lives of millions of ordinary people who believe in the Lord Jesus and who have received his Spirit. This is bringing about a major transformation in the Church with a shift away from the domination of the professional clergy. This is the day of the laity. This is the day of the ordinary people, made extraordinary through the Spirit of God which is being poured out in abundance, just as Joel foresaw.

It is not only the Church as a whole which is being transformed but the individual lives of those people who are discovering that they can do things which they would previously have thought impossible. They recognise, however, that their newly-found power comes from God and is not due to personal achievement. This ensures that all the glory goes to the Lord and not to themselves. This is no doubt one of the reasons why God delights to raise up the humble poor, who know they could do nothing in their own strength but who are entirely dependent on him.

Paul continually praised God that it was in his times of greatest weakness that he found the greatest strength of the Lord poured out upon his life. "I can do everything through him who gives me strength" he boasted (Philippians 4:13). Paul was able to say, "When I am weak, then I am strong". He even saw this as the reason why God had not healed his body, because God had said to him, "My grace is sufficient for you, for my power is made perfect in weakness" (2 Corinthians 12:9–10). This is the wonderful experience being discovered by millions of believers today through the great outpouring of the Spirit of God.

4. Male/Female Partnership

One of the major features of the prophecy of Joel was that both men and women would be filled with the Spirit. This would break one of the tragic effects of the Fall seen in the male dominance that has characterised male/female relationships ever since that time. Joel foresaw that the outpouring of the Spirit of God would restore the natural harmony of creation, wherein God had created both men and women in his own image and given them authority together over the whole created order. Joel's words imply a time coming when men would no longer lord it over women, just as Jesus told his disciples that they were not to "lord it over one another". Relationships among believers were to be of an entirely different order to those pertaining in the world.

The Twentieth Century has seen a major shift towards the fulfilment of this vision of equality between the sexes in the Church. Some churches, such as the Congregational and Presbyterian, have been ordaining women for more than a century. Major steps have been taken more recently by most of the mainline churches, including Anglicans, particularly in the USA, towards full equality between men and women in ministry.

In America, Pentecostals have led the way towards equality in ministry. In the USA one third of all female ordinations are reported to occur in Pentecostal churches.

women, though, still represent only a small minority of those ordained into the pastoral ministry; for example, eleven per cent of those ordained in the Assemblies of God in the USA are women, and twelve per cent in the Church of God in Christ. In other denominations the percentage of women entering their ministries has risen dramatically during the past decade. It is estimated that by the year 2000 approximately a quarter of all the pastors in the mainline denominations in the USA will be women.

There are no comparable statistics available for Britain, but the number of those entering the pastoral ministry of the mainline churches is probably not very different. Despite the recognition within the charismatic movement of the gifts of the Holy Spirit being available to all people regardless of wealth, education or sex, most of the newer charismatic churches have lagged behind the mainline denominations in the matter of sex equality in all forms of ministry. Their practices of male leadership are usually based upon a literal application of statements on the position of women in the Pauline Epistles. Leaders in the mainline charismatic churches have usually recognised the need to interpret Paul's statements with regard to women in the same context as his advice concerning slavery. Paul was anxious to defend the infant Church against any charges of political or social subversion, but his ideal for the community of believers is seen in his basic Gospel pronouncement: "There is neither Jew nor Greek, slave nor free, male nor female, for you are all one in Christ Jesus" (Galatians 3:28).

Women have been in leadership positions on the overseas mission field, sent out by churches from Europe and North America, for more than a century. Many of these would not have been permitted to exercise the same authority in their home churches, but today the recognition of the roles that women play in wider society, in politics, in law, in medicine, in social caring, in teaching and in every other sphere of human activity, has challenged the churches to reassess their own commitment to equality between the sexes.

The ideal is not simply one of equality but of partnership where each has different gifts. In the New Testament this ideal is seen in such partnerships in ministry as that of Priscilla and Aquila. The outpouring of the Spirit upon both men and women adds a spiritual dimension that sanctifies the different attributes each one brings to the task of ministry. This in turn is not only bringing a broader range of leadership skills into the Church, but is enabling a significant movement to take place towards the recognition of "lay ministries" and the equipping of all believers.

There is an increasing trend towards partnership ministries in most churches today, replacing the old "one-man-band" type of pastoral ministry, where one man was expected to exercise all the ministry gifts. The ideal partnership includes both men and women with their different abilities. It is interesting to note in Paul's teaching on the fruit of the Spirit, that most of the attributes he lists are traditionally female (Galatians 5:22–23). Men may sometimes have been known for their love and joy; but certainly not for peace, patience, kindness, goodness, fidelity or gentleness (or possibly even self-control!). The "macho" image would list a completely different set of attributes; but the fruit of the Spirit which Paul expected to see in all believers, both men and women, was in strong contrast.

On the day of Pentecost, Peter saw Joel's vision beginning to be fulfilled as the Holy Spirit descended upon the 120 believers, men and women of all ages and from different strata of society. The concept of all believers, regardless of differences in sex, social status, age or even ability, being filled with the Spirit of God, is the vision presented in scripture for the coming of the Kingdom of God. It is in striking contrast to the values of the world where women are exploited and the poor are ignored. It contrasts especially with the practices of Islam where women are oppressed and the poor are despised.

It is for this reason that the Gospel is being received as "good news" by millions of the world's poorest and most oppressed people, especially by those suffering under the joyless oppression of Islam. Jesus saw his own mission as being sent by the Father to "proclaim freedom for the prisoners" and "to release the oppressed" (Luke 4:18). His followers were to continue this mission and the Holy Spirit is being poured out upon all believers today to enable them to do this.

5. *The Power of the Holy Spirit*

The whole of the Acts of the Apostles bears testimony to the power of the Holy Spirit and the transforming effect upon the lives of ordinary people. This is being seen today, and is a major sign of the new prophetic movement. God is fulfilling his promise to give the power of his Spirit to all people and thus bring glory to his name.

Jesus warned his disciples not to attempt to do the work of God by human strength. The Great Commission, commanding them to go out to all the world carrying the Gospel to all nations, was followed by the strategy that Jesus gave to the disciples in Acts 1:8. But he was careful to precede this with the warning not to leave Jerusalem until the power of the Spirit which the Father had promised, had come upon them.

This power was undoubtedly envisaged by Joel, and it was certainly in the understanding of Peter as he emphasised the prophetic role they would exercise with the words "and they will prophesy". Today we are seeing this become a reality in the mighty deeds being performed by ordinary people through the power of the Holy Spirit. Quite clearly the things that are happening today could not be performed through human strength, but only through supernatural strength.

There are multitudes of stories abounding today from every part of the world that reveal the way God is fulfilling his promise and bringing great glory to his name through the power of the Spirit working in the lives of ordinary people. The great revival that is currently sweeping through Indonesia, the largest Muslim state in the world, began in East Timor in 1965 in the midst of the bloodiest revolution ever to assail that part of the world. The revival began among simple peasant farmers, most of whom were illiterate. They had heard of Jesus, and knew of his promises, and they began taking him at his word. As they laid hands on the sick and prayed for them, amazing miracles took place. They discovered too that God would actually reveal to them things they could not possibly have known through human wisdom, such as the presence of demonic spirits, and he also gave them the authority to deal with them in the name of Jesus.

The power of God is still to be seen in Indonesia, in some amazing ways that confound human reason, when the Gospel is preached among animistic tribal groups. The fetishes swallowed in pagan practices, and the needles inserted under the skin as part of these rites, are often violently ejected at the time of conversion. The images of idols are vomited and needles come out from under the skin and can be heard falling to the ground without any act of will on the part of the new believer. This is a clear and dramatic demonstration of the power of the Holy Spirit to overcome and drive out evil spirits.

In our travels throughout South-East Asia we have both heard and seen the power of the Holy Spirit at work among the people. In China, where Christians have been persecuted for forty years and where, even today, there are strong restrictions upon the churches, there are multitudes of stories of the courage and faith of believers. Typical is the account, given to us by a pastor in Guangzhou, of two teen-age girls who were attacked by three men in a field who were bent on raping them as they were making their way home one evening. They cried out to the Lord for protection and the three men all fell to the ground. The girls ran on to their village and told their pastor who, together with one of the elders, hurried out to the field and found the men still lying there. They prayed over them and the men sat up. The pastor told them that the Lord had struck them down and worse things would befall them if they did not repent. They immediately gave their lives to Christ. News of what had happened spread through the village and surrounding area. The conversion of the three men, who were notorious for their evil lives, astounded everyone and resulted in many others coming to the Lord.

When the power of God is seen in such dramatic ways it demonstrates the presence of the Lord among his people and his willingness to answer their pleas for help. It also shows the faith of ordinary believers and the power of God available to them through the outpouring of the Holy Spirit such as we are seeing today.

6. An Issachar Generation

Another sign of the rise of a new prophetic movement in our day is to be seen in the widespread recognition among Christians of the significance of events in the contemporary world.

In the time when David was recognised as king by all the tribes of Israel, there was one tribe who exercised this particular spiritual insight – the tribe of Issachar. In 1 Chronicles 12, there is an account of representatives of each of the tribes coming to David at Hebron to declare their loyalty to him. Verse 32 records the particular gift of the men of Issachar "who understood the times and knew what Israel should do".

In later times in Israel, this was the role of the prophets. They were the "watchmen" of the nation who studied both international and national trends, and especially had the task of interpreting what God was saying to the people both through his deeds and through direct revelation of his word. This was the essential nature of the prophetic task and any prophetic movement today will bear these characteristics. Prophecy has the two-way responsibility of hearing from God through divine revelation and declaring it in ways and words that are understandable to the people.

The prophets were also the intercessors of the nation who continually got into the presence of God to seek his face on behalf of his people. This also needed to be two-way – listening to God and speaking to him. There is today much evidence of a recovery of this two-way relationship in prayer, with an emphasis upon the necessity of listening to God and of acting as watchmen for the Lord and studying his word in scripture. All of these are marks of a true prophetic movement and are signs of the fulfilment of the vision of Joel.

God is looking for an "Issachar people" who are prepared to spend time studying his word in scripture and acting as "watchmen upon the walls" in the towns and cities where they live, so that they can observe carefully what is happening and spread it before the Lord to receive an understanding of what the Spirit is saying to the churches today. The Issachar people are the prophets in their local communities, and their emergence today is both a fulfilment of the wish of Moses for all the people to be prophets and of the vision seen by Joel.

7. Radical Witness

The prophets of Israel were always radical in their witness and their declaration of the word of God. They challenged the status quo; they were disturbers of society rather than those who exercised a maintenance ministry. This was no doubt the reason why there was always antipathy between priests and prophets. The priests' role was primarily to maintain tradition, whereas the prophets were liable to challenge any practice, however hallowed by tradition. Their task was to question whether the practice was really what was required by God in that day. They saw that God required his people to walk by faith, and not simply by tradition, so that they would trust him afresh for the changing demands of changing circumstances.

The witness of the prophets was also closely allied to the nature of God. As God revealed to them that an essential part of his nature was justice, or mercy or love, so the prophets applied this to the circumstances of the day. If they failed to see justice in human relationships in the life of the nation, they were able to declare the word of the Lord with boldness because God had revealed to them that this was what he required of his people, including those in leadership positions. Hence Isaiah was able to speak scathingly to the rich who added "house to house" and joined "field to field" (5:8). And he was able to declare that the kind of fasting that God wanted to see was "to loose the chains of injustice" and "to set the oppressed free" and "to share your food with the hungry" (58:6 and 7).

Today we are seeing a fresh emphasis upon these basic requirements of God in human relationships; this is an essential part of a prophetic witness. The social gospel, that was an outcome of Nineteenth-Century radicalism, was despised by evangelicals in the first half of this century because it became largely detached from the basic requirements of the Gospel in the life-changing experience of conversion. Today, that imbalance is being corrected through a large-scale movement among evangelicals demonstrating their concern for the poor, for the deprived, for social justice and for equality in social and racial relationships. The Evangelical Alliance in Britain and the Evangelicals for Social Action (ESA) in the USA have been foremost in spearheading this evangelical radicalism.

This movement can be seen in a commitment to inner-city ministries as well as to overseas mission. More recently it has included a growing concern for global issues in a wide variety of fields including political, economic and ecological.

The correcting of the imbalance in the Church between those who wanted the kingdom without the King and others who wanted the King without the kingdom, is of prophetic significance. It is an indication that the new prophetic movement gaining momentum today is in line with the basic biblical concept of prophecy.

As the Spirit of God is poured out in fulfilment of the prophecy of Joel, so millions of the world's poor are being swept into the kingdom. Increasingly, their voice is being heard with the prophetic call for justice that one day will have to be heeded, even in the corridors of power of the world's richest nations.

8. Commitment to Evangelism

Peter's statement "and they shall prophesy", when he saw what was happening on the day of Pentecost, was no doubt linked in his own mind with the fulfilment of the Great Commission that the Gospel should be preached to all peoples in all the nations. It is the intention of God that in the last days his word should be declared throughout the world, and in order to fulfil his purposes he is empowering ordinary people to share their faith. The great evangelistic campaigns that have characterised the past century, have largely been man-directed, whereas God promises to do it *his way* in the "last days" through an outpouring of the Spirit of God upon all people.

We are seeing today, as part of the new prophetic movement, the urge to evangelise on the part of ordinary people who love the Lord Jesus and who long to share with others their own joy and the power they have discovered in their new relationship with God through Christ. This urge to evangelise can most clearly be seen in the non-industrialised nations, especially where the Gospel has become indigenised and freed from the cultural contamination of the western nations.

In the western industrialised nations, there is a new awareness of the need for conversion. For many centuries the necessity for a conversion experience has not been highlighted in nations where the vast majority of the population were Christian (at least nominally). Parents promised to bring up their children in the Christian faith and to nurture them "in the love and admonition of the Lord", thus the emphasis was upon the pastoral role of the Church, and evangelism was relegated to overseas mission. Today, after a century of secularism, conversion is again on the agenda of most churches for local mission.

Church planting has become a characteristic of renewal today not simply in the Pentecostal and House Church movements but even among Anglicans. Faith sharing is being encouraged in churches of all denominations as part of the shift away from clergy and professional ministers to laity. There is widespread recognition that it is the ordinary people who are on the front line of mission today.

This was what was foreseen by Peter when he referred to the prophecy of Joel and the worldwide outpouring of the Spirit of God. Those upon whom the Spirit fell would not simply rejoice in the gifts of God for themselves; they would be impelled to share their faith with others. They would not be able to keep quiet. They would have to declare the wonderful works of God which would be seen in their commitment to evangelism and to carrying the Gospel to all peoples everywhere.

9. Mounting Opposition

Any new move of God is always accompanied by increased opposition from those who, for a variety of reasons, find it unacceptable. The Pentecostal/charismatic movement throughout the Twentieth Century has had its opponents within the Church, but today that opposition is decreasing as the renewal movement gains in acceptability. The wilder excesses of charismatic fervour are less in evidence, while the deeper spiritual significance of renewal is running through most avenues of church life.

The major opposition to the Spirit of God moving within the churches today is coming from counterfeit spiritual forces. The rising interest in the occult in secular society is having its effect upon the Church, with satanists deliberately opposing the Gospel, and other milder forms of spiritism infiltrating the Church. The New Age movement is gaining momentum within the Church as well as outside, and this may well result in the persecution of believers in the future.

The main opposition today is, however, from outside the Church rather than from within, especially from the forces of secular humanism. For most of the century, the greatest organised opposition to the Gospel has come from Communist atheistic states. In the USSR it is estimated that nearly seventy million people were killed in the seventy years between 1917 and 1987. It is not suggested that these were all Christian martyrs. They were the victims of political purges, but with the known opposition of Communist officials to any form of religion, those who professed faith or were suspected of being believers, were prime targets. We can only conclude that an unknown number of the millions who lost their lives between the Communist Revolution and *perestroika* were martyrs for the Lord Jesus. In China similarly the vast majority of those killed were not Christians, since there were less than one million believers in the whole of China in 1949. But we know now that millions became believers during the years of persecution, so we can only conclude that China has seen an unknown number of Christian martyrs.

There has been a significant shift in recent years from Communism to Islam as the chief opponent of the Gospel. Muslims are not known for their respect of life, and the *Qur'an* actually encourages the elimination of Christians and Jews. The rise of Islamic fundamentalism is a significant development which threatens to divide the world and could result in a "Holy War". There is pressure from Muslim leaders in a number of nations to introduce *Sharia* (Islamic law) which is increasing the division between Muslims and Christians in countries such as Nigeria.

There are now at least seventy nations closed to foreign missions. These are mostly countries dominated by Islam, and in many of them any form of evangelism is strictly prohibited and there are open attacks upon Christians. The number of known Christian martyrs today is estimated by David Barrett to have escalated to 300,000 believers losing their lives each year.

There is prophetic significance in the rising number of Christian martyrs which is an indication of the willingness of believers to make the ultimate sacrifice for their faith. The witness of martyrs is always powerful and has an effect upon unbelievers as well as believers, and is thus an aid to evangelism and the growth of the Church, as it has been in China. Persecution also has the additional effect of bringing about a purified Church, since only those who are prepared to take an uncompromising stand for the faith remain in it.

Martyrdom is ultimately the most powerful form of prophecy. Just as the prophets of Israel did not prophesy only in words, but also in deeds, so the act of laying down one's life for the sake of the Lord is the most powerful form of declaring the Gospel. It is a mark of the new prophetic movement.

10. The Breaking Down of Barriers

The far-reaching changes that have been seen gaining momentum throughout this century have had a radical effect upon Christian mission and the growth of the Church. The political changes that have taken place at such an amazing pace in Eastern Europe and the Soviet Union in the last half of the 1980s have considerable significance for Christian mission.

Rightly perceived, these changes are not simply the results of economic pressures or changes in the political climate, they are in fact the fulfilment of prophecy. God is carrying out his promises to shake the nations and to bring forth a great harvest for the kingdom. God always fulfils his purposes in his own way and it is his intention that the Gospel should reach the peoples of all nations and tribes and languages and cultures.

The barriers to the Gospel inevitably fall when God begins to act in fulfilment of his declared intentions. That is what we are seeing today and that is why the political changes that have begun to transform the social geography of the world are of prophetic significance. In all the former Communist countries of Eastern Europe, there is a resurgence of evangelism as the new openness to the Gospel begins to give fresh opportunity to Christians to declare their faith. Just as in China after the death of Mao Tse Tung and the release of Christians from prison, there was a resurgence of faith among the believers, so today in Eastern Europe and throughout Russia there are similar stirrings among the faithful. Even in Albania, the only European nation still ruled by Communists and closed to the Gospel, there are signs of hope. It is no longer illegal to profess a faith even though evangelism is still prohibited.

Many of the *barriers* within the churches that have been a hindrance to the Gospel are slowly breaking down, such as the old spirit of denominationalism that has kept Christians apart for centuries. The new unity movement engendered through renewal is a movement which is more spiritual than institutional and is coming from a ground swell at grassroots level rather than as a result of leadership decisions. This again is a further indication of God fulfilling his purposes in his own way and is a result of the outpouring of the Spirit upon all people.

11. Heightened Expectation

Further evidence of the new prophetic movement is to be seen in the strong sense of expectation found among believers throughout the world today. This expectation is taking many forms and is not always based upon a sound interpretation of scripture, but it is an expectation of God's activity in a world increasingly dominated by fear of the terrible consequences of man's own actions. Vast numbers of Christians today are reacting against global threats to the peace and security of the world and to the health of the planet by turning to God in a new way as the only hope for humanity.

There is a rise in the expectation of divine intervention into the affairs of the world. This may take the form of the Rapture, or of the Second Coming of Christ, or the hope of revival sweeping across all nations; but increasingly believers are turning to God and seeking *his* solution to the problems besetting the nations. "Christ the Hope of the World" is not simply a popular conference theme but is becoming, not only the way of salvation, but also of survival.

The new sense of expectation among Christians is a result of millions of ordinary believers experiencing the gifts of the Spirit and coming into a personal relationship with the Lord. This has raised the level of faith which is reflected in the popularity of celebration events and large gatherings where the emphasis is upon praise and worship. There is also the expectation of God speaking to his people, which has had a dramatic effect upon the prayer life of the Church and the rise of intercessory groups right across the world. This expectation is, therefore, a genuine mark of God empowering his people to prophesy since we have to receive the word of God through divine revelation in order to be able to declare it.

12. Prophetic Boldness

A major sign of a new prophetic movement is when the word of God is declared with great boldness and with a power and authority that clearly comes from God himself. There is evidence from all over the world that this is happening as believers grow in confidence that they are hearing from the Lord and as the signs of his presence among his people multiply.

The rapidly changing events on the world scene, political, economic and ecological, have created an increasing sense of urgency among Christians in every part of the world, especially among those who are familiar with biblical prophecy. As the end of the second millennium draws nearer there are tremendous drives towards world evangelisation. The 1990s have been declared a "Decade of Evangelism" and there is a desire among those involved in mission organisations to present the Lord Jesus with a "Two thousandth birthday present" of half the world's population as believers and members of his Church.

It is, however, not only leaders who are becoming increasingly bold in their declaration of the truth as they believe God is revealing it to them, but also multitudes of ordinary believers who perceive how God is at work in the world today and who are seizing every opportunity to speak of their faith. It is this witness of the people that is the most powerful force for evangelism today and despite the mounting opposition to the Gospel in many parts of the world, there is an increasing boldness in the witness of Christians. Fearlessness in the face of opposition comes as a result of absolute confidence in the Lord and his ability to fulfil his word. The key to this fearlessness lies in hearing from God. Thus the new prophetic movement with its stress upon listening to the Lord and contemporary divine revelation is of the utmost significance in building the faith of believers.

We have seen many examples of this "prophetic boldness" in those whom we have met in our ministry around the world. There are none more fearless than those who face the constant opposition of determined and ruthless authorities. The witness of Pastor Samuel Lam, whose story is told in *Rich Christians, Poor Christians*, has had an outstanding impact throughout China and South East Asia. Since the massacre of students in Tiananman Square and the tightening of the screw on the unregistered churches, he has experienced renewed persecution but as he said to us "after twenty-two years in prison, they have done everything they can to me except take my life – and I am ready for that".

Another outstanding Christian in South-East Asia, whom we have come to respect as a prophetic leader and personal friend, is Dr Petrus Octavianus of Indonesia. He is an evangelist who has been responsible for tens of thousands coming to Christ. On one occasion he had rented an openair sports stadium for an evangelistic campaign, despite the opposition of the local Islamic authorities. Many Muslims came to the meeting determined to create trouble and were already making a disturbance in the crowd before Petrus spoke. His anxieties were increased by thick black clouds appearing in the sky over the city, and it was obvious that a downpour of rain was imminent. This would not only have scattered the crowd and caused the abandonment of the meeting but would have been seen by the Imams as a triumph of Allah over Christ and would have been a great setback to the spread of the Gospel in that part of Indonesia.

Petrus cried out to the Lord asking him to defend the honour of his name. To his amazement, he heard the Lord say, "Command the clouds to disperse, and I will protect this stadium and all who are in it from the storm". Petrus was overjoyed to hear this, and with eyes closed he silently obeyed then looked expectantly up into the sky. But instead of seeing the clouds break, the first drops of rain began to fall! Again he silently cried out to the Lord for help. Then the instruction came once again, "Command the clouds to disperse, and I will protect this stadium and all who are in it from the storm". He realised that the Lord was telling him to declare the word publicly in the hearing of all the people and he would see the miracle God was promising.

In fear and trembling, yet with great boldness, he stepped forward to the microphone and commanded the clouds to disperse and the storm to go away "in the Name of the Lord Jesus". Suddenly the black clouds parted and the sunshine streamed down upon the stadium. They could hear heavy rain falling across the city but the stadium remained dry. The effect upon the crowd was startling. Hundreds fell onto their faces on the ground as the fear of the Lord overwhelmed them. Petrus was given great boldness to declare the Gospel and to say that the Lord Jesus who had stilled the storm on the Sea of Galilee is still Lord of all Creation today and that there is "salvation in no other Name". The Muslim trouble-makers were utterly confounded and silenced.

They listened with great attention to the Gospel and many hundreds became believers that day.

This is the prophetic boldness which is given to the Lord's servants today – to those who listen to him, who trust him and who dare to take him at his word. Neither Samuel Lam, nor Petrus Octavianus, would claim to be either Pentecostal or charismatic, but they are simply believers in the Lord Jesus, who have the anointing of the Spirit of God upon their lives, and who have learned how to get into the presence of God, and whose faith enables them to declare the word of the Lord with great boldness. This surely is a sign of a genuine prophetic movement through which God is fulfilling his promise to pour out his Spirit in abundant measure upon his people.

We see the emerging signs of this new prophetic movement that is gaining momentum around the world today in each of the aspects we have noted briefly in this chapter. They are:

The Worldwide Growth of the Church which is a sign of the harvest of the kingdom.

The Lordship of Jesus being acknowledged in the lives of his people.

Ordinary People Spirit-Filled, not just the leaders, but the humble poor raised up by God.

Male/Female Partnership in contrast to the values of the world.

The Power of the Holy Spirit being seen working through the lives of believers.

An Issachar Generation who are both watchmen and intercessors.

Radical Witness being made by believers causing the message of the biblical prophets to be heard today.

Commitment to Evangelism is being seen among people in all the nations.

Mounting Opposition to the Gospel is accompanying

the fresh move of God.

The Breaking Down of Barriers to the Gospel in many nations and between denominations.

Heightened Expectation of believers that God is fulfilling his promises to his people.

Prophetic Boldness of believers who have the Spirit of God upon them.

The worldwide prophetic movement that can be seen today is the work of God himself fulfilling his purposes declared of old through the prophets and apostles. God is fulfilling his purposes in his own way, not according to the expectations or methods of the world. What we have been noting throughout this book, and have summarised in this chapter, is in strong contrast to what is being spoken of as a new "prophetic movement" by some leaders in the western church. Their emphasis is upon signs and wonders, and their teaching leads people to believe that they will exercise supernatural power to gain dominance in secular society. We see these teachings and expectations as being heavily influenced by worldly values and as having little to do with the true prophetic movement initiated by God through the outpouring of his Spirit.

Azusa Street Prophecy

In 1906, during the early days of the Twentieth Century Pentecostal movement, a prophecy was given at Azusa Street, Los Angeles saying that the day would come when the works of the flesh would hinder the work of the Spirit. The prophecy said that:

"In the last days three things will happen in the great Pentecostal movement:
1. There will be an overemphasis on power rather

than on righteousness.

2. There will be an overemphasis on praise to a God they no longer pray to.
3. There will be an overemphasis on the gifts of the Spirit rather than on the Lordship of Christ.

In the western charismatic churches today there is certainly a strong emphasis upon power and as we have already noted the desire for power is often a desire of the flesh that is self-centred and man-centred rather than Christ-centred. There is certainly a lot of talk today about "holiness" and an emphasis upon right standards of personal behaviour which is much needed in the churches; but even here there is a danger of this becoming inward-looking in contrast to the biblical stress upon right relationships. This misunderstanding of "righteousness" is by no means confined to the charismatic churches, neither is it a modern phenomenon; it stems from the western church taking over the Roman legalistic approach to righteousness which dates back to the Early Church.

Paul's references to "righteousness" were always in the context of its Hebrew links with "justice". Throughout the Bible, in both Old and New Testaments, the terms "righteousness" and "justice" are interchangeable in almost every instance. The just man was one who was in a right relationship with God and with his neighbours. Thus righteousness in the Bible was never the privatised concept that it has become today in western evangelical interpretation which allows evangelicals to lose sight of their responsibilities for their local community, their nation and for the world while concentrating upon their personal morality and their standing in the eyes of God.

The second point in the Azusa Street prophecy was "an over-emphasis upon praise". It is arguable that we can never over-emphasise praise because however much we praise the Lord he is worthy of still more. But this prophecy clearly refers to a time when the praises of men will be empty and meaningless as in the time of Isaiah, when God said, "These people come near to me with their mouth and honour me with their lips, but their hearts are far from me" (Isaiah 29:13). Praise in many fellowships today is certainly enthusiastic and exuberant with the aid of many powerful electronic musical instruments and drums. But sometimes the Lord says "Away with the noise of your songs! I will not listen to the music of your harps. But let justice roll on like a river, righteousness like a never-failing stream!" (Amos 5:23–24).

God looks upon our hearts and not at the outward appearance. He does not judge our praises by the volume or the quality of the melody or even by the words. He knows what is in our hearts, however poorly we express our love and praises. There is certainly a great emphasis upon prayer today which we have already noted, but it is not always those who are most vocal in praise or active in "praise marches" or "praise celebrations" who are foremost in intercession. Even the intercessors themselves need to make sure that they really know the God to whom they are praying.

The Azusa Street prophecy also referred to "an over-emphasis on the gifts of the Spirit rather than the Lordship of Christ". Certainly today there is a great emphasis upon the gifts of the Spirit and much teaching on the subject. The danger of this emphasis is where the gifts are desired for themselves rather than seen as being bestowed by God upon his servants for the working out of his purpose in and through the Church. Rightly understood the gifts are not the *possession* of individuals but *manifestations* of the Spirit of God coming upon one who is in a right relationship with the Lord.

We see the recognition of the Lordship of Christ as one of the signs of the new prophetic movement, but it is more in evidence in non-western nations. The acknowledgement of the Lordship of Christ is essential if we are to have the right attitude towards spiritual gifts. It ensures not only our own humility and recognition of our absolute dependence upon the Lord, but it also ensures that he, and he alone, is given all the glory.

The three elements in the Azusa Street prophecy taken together indicate a strong warning concerning the dangers of the flesh getting into the Church and prostituting the work of the Holy Spirit.

There are certainly many indications today that the western churches are heavily influenced by the desires of the flesh and the self-centred materialism of Western society. It appears that one half of the Pentecostal/charismatic churches are waiting for the Rapture, and the other half are expecting to exercise dominion over the nations! This, of course, is a caricature, but the point we are emphasising is that many believers have opted out of responsibility for doing anything about the state of the world. They are only interested in personal salvation in the expectation that Christ will take them out of the world before anything unpleasant happens.

The other half are so excited about the prospect of revival and the expectation that they will exercise power and authority to rule the nations, that they have lost sight of the cost of revival. They are, therefore, missing the essential prerequisites for the outpouring of the Spirit of God which are *repentance* and *brokenness*. We have to be broken not only of desires but of trust in the flesh before God can use us in any mighty work of the Spirit. The humble poor in the Third World nations do not need to be told this. It is one of those things that God has revealed to those who have no worldly power or status but who simply love him and trust him through Jesus their Saviour.

The Church in the West is under tremendous attack today, both from the pressures of the world and the flesh getting into the things of the Spirit and also from the subtleties of New Age teaching penetrating the churches. We see all this as an attack from the principalities and powers who are seeking to overthrow the work of God by distorting the truth and deceiving the people.

A Close Walk With God

The only safeguard against deception is the right relationship with God that comes from a humble and contrite heart. The whole Bible bears witness to the fundamental truth that humility is the key to a close walk with God. Moses was said to be a very humble man, "more humble than anyone else on the face of the earth" (Numbers 12:3) and God said that he spoke with his servant Moses face to face (Numbers 12:8).

Jesus linked humility and purity of heart with a right relationship with God. He said it is the meek who will inherit the earth and "blessed are the pure in heart, for they will see God" (Matthew 5:5–8). When we truly love the Lord we also love his word which enables us to understand the nature and purposes of God and his ways. Our love of the Lord and our trust in him brings about an openness that will allow God to work out his purposes through our lives – to do his work, and to do it *his* way!

The Testimony of Jesus

The testimony of Jesus was that he did nothing on his own initiative. This should be our objective in following the Lord Jesus. Jesus repeated his testimony on numerous occasions. He said, "The Son can do nothing by himself; he can only do what he sees his Father doing . . . for the Father loves the Son and shows him all he does" (John 5:19–20). Jesus learned to keep his eyes upon the Father and to watch what he was doing. He also learned to listen to the Father: He said "By myself I can do nothing; I judge only as I hear, and my judgement is just, for I seek not to please myself but him who sent me" (John 5:30).

From these two sayings we learn that Jesus communicated with the Father in the same way as did the prophets – through seeing and hearing. Throughout his life Jesus spent much time alone with the Father. He would get up early before dawn and go up into the hills in Galilee to pray, and on occasions he would spend whole nights in prayer when he was seeking to know the will of the Father for important decisions in his ministry such as the choosing of the Twelve.

A further important part of Jesus' testimony was that he sought never to please himself but always to please his Father. It was for this reason that he did nothing on his own initiative. He declared, "I do nothing on my own but speak just what the Father has taught me . . . for I always do what pleases him" (John 8:28–29). Jesus paid such close attention to what the Father was saying to him that he not only spoke the words the Father gave him but he said them in exactly the way the Father intended. He testified, "For I did not speak of my own accord, but the Father who sent me commanded me what to say and how to say it. . . . Whatever I say is just what the Father told me to say" (John 12:49–50).

When speaking to his own disciples he went even farther and said, "The words I say to you are not just my own. Rather, it is the Father, living in me, who is doing his work" (John 14:10). The teaching of Jesus is that we too can hear from God and know what he is saying to us. He said, "He who belongs to God, hears what God says" (John 8:47). The secret lies in the closeness of our relationship with him.

Jesus used the illustration of the shepherd and the sheep where the sheep actually recognised the voice of their own shepherd. It was a common practice for several flocks to be brought together into the same pen, which made it easier for the shepherds to guard them through the night by sleeping near the gate of the sheepfold. In the morning the gate would be opened and each shepherd would call to his own sheep and they would recognise his voice and follow him. In referring to this, Jesus said, "The watchman opens the gate for him, and the sheep listen to his voice. He calls his own sheep by name and leads them out . . . his sheep follow him because they know his voice". Jesus had also observed the fact, that "they will never follow a stranger; in fact, they will run away from him because they do not recognise a stranger's voice". He gave this assurance "I am the Good Shepherd; I know my sheep and my sheep know me . . . they will listen to my voice" (John 10:1–18).

Learning to listen to the Lord is probably the most needed thing in the Church today. Without this listening ear, such as the prophet Samuel had even as a young man, we cannot know what God is saying to us and therefore we cannot be fully obedient to him. If we don't know what he is requiring of us, how can we do what he asks? It is for this reason that we need to pay particular attention not only to the teaching of Jesus but to his own personal testimony of how he watched what the Father was doing and listened for his word so that he not only knew what to say but even how to say it.

This is the testimony of Jesus, and scripture tells us that "the testimony of Jesus is the spirit of prophecy" (Revelation 19:10). As the testimony of Jesus becomes our testimony so the Spirit of the Lord Jesus is poured out on his people and they are enabled to declare the wonderful works of God and to bring glory to his Name so that the prophecy of Joel is fulfilled.

. . . AND THEY SHALL PROPHESY!